The Conspiracy of the Text

Social Worlds of Childhood

General Editor: Rom Harré

The Conspiracy of the Text

The Place of Narrative in the Development of Thought

Jeff Adams

Routledge & Kegan Paul
London and New York

To my Mother and the memory of my Father

First published in 1986
by Routledge & Kegan Paul plc
11 New Fetter Lane, London EC4P 4EE
Published in the USA by
Routledge & Kegan Paul Inc.
in association with Methuen Inc.
29 West 35th Street, New York, NY 10001

Set in Monotype Times Roman
and printed in Great Britain
by Butler & Tanner Ltd
Frome and London

Library of Congress Cataloging in Publication Data
Adams, Jeff.
   The conspiracy of the text.
   (Social worlds of childhood)
   Bibliography: p.
   Includes index.
   1. Reading, Psychology of.   2. Reading comprehension.
3. Thought and thinking.   4. Discourse analysis,
Narrative.   5. Beauty and the beast (Tale)—Psychological
aspects.   I. Title.   II. Series.
BF456.R2A33   1986   153.6   85–25705
ISBN 0-7102-0799-9

Contents

vi   *Contents*

General Editor's Preface

For most of us childhood is a forgotten and even a rejected time. The aim of this series is to recover the flavour of childhood and adolescence in a systematic and sympathetic way. The frame of mind cultivated by the authors as investigators is that of anthropologists who glimpse a strange tribe across a space of forest and millennia of time. The huddled group on the other side of the school playground and the thumping of feet in the upstairs rooms mark the presence of a strange tribe. This frame of mind is deliberately different from that of the classical investigators of child psychology, who have brought adult concepts to bear upon the understanding of children's thoughts and actions, and have looked at childhood primarily as a passage towards the skills and accomplishments and distortions of adults. In these studies the authors try to look upon the activities of children as autonomous and complete in themselves. Of course, not all the activities of childhood could be treated in this way. Rather than being in opposition to the traditional kind of study, the work upon which this series is based aims to amplify our understanding by bringing to light aspects of childhood which usually remain invisible when it is looked at in the traditional way. The ethnogenic method is in use throughout the studies represented in this series, that is the children themselves are the prime sources of theories about their actions and thoughts and of explanations of the inwardness of their otherwise mysterious activities.

Part I

The Structure of the Text and the Process of Reading

Introduction

This book is about human understanding. The focal point for it is the process of reading. The material used to develop the theory put forward here is children's readings of fairy tales. But this book is not primarily concerned with children; they are a means to an end which is to answer the question: 'What does it mean to read?'

One of my concerns for a number of years has been determining how a meaning or sense can be grasped from a text. Text can be taken in a very broad sense including, for example, novels, television programs, newspapers or, indeed, fairy tales. Coupled with this interest has been the obvious affective attachment that readers have for their texts. Thus, for example, the fact that a child *needs* to hear or read a particular story at a particular time indicates that there is an attachment there of interest.

An adult example of this is newspaper readership and allegiance. There are certain newspapers I cannot buy and only one that I am attached to which I actually miss, 'feel the lack of', when its distribution is interrupted in one way or another. I suspect that many people need some sort of 'accepted' daily ideological input, and *one* of the problems that must face the bulk of the British press is trying to distinguish ideological/affective styles to determine the difference that makes a difference.

But 'texts' are only part of the solution to understanding reading. One also has to look at readers; particular readers for particular texts. This is one of the main reasons for looking at child readers. Bettelheim (1978) has produced an exhaustive and convincing study of the meaning of fairy tales. This work opened up a lot of possibilities and, although he was concerned with the texts and their psycho-analytic bases, it occurred to me that what the child makes of the current favourite story, how and why it is used, would make a fruitful area for investigating the understanding problem.

Reading is conceived here as a 'clash' of structures: that of the imagination of the reader rooted in personal circumstance and the structure of the text situated in the language.

It is important for me *not* to describe the text using adult readings, such as Bettelheim's, but rather to try to describe and account for *what the child reader is faced with*. My answer is briefly that the reader, at rock bottom, is faced with a narrative system of signs, based on conventions for communication; i.e. a semiotic system. The text is faced with a reader situated in, to use Bettelheim's phrase, existential predicaments; the reader is not an idealised person but a growing citizen.

So what is the effect of one on the other? The text, I will argue, conspires with the language to direct readings which are appropriate to the culture while the reader struggles to use the text for personal ends. It is by listening to the reader within the systems of signification of the text that this process can be revealed.

If reading is meaningful *to* someone, then it must have an affective base and consequently the '/' between cognition and affect can be seen as misleading and without doubt, as I hope to show, an obsolete and misconceived methodological necessity.

The structure that clashes with the text will simply be called 'thought' for it is hard to conceive of affectless thought or thoughtless affect when we discuss reading or understanding and, as I will show, writing as well. As Bertold Brecht said: 'We think feelingly and feel thoughtfully.' This theme underlies much of what follows.

The book is divided into two parts. The first is a theoretical section which develops ideas which lead to a model of text grammar and what it means to read. The second section shows how the theory of reading and text structure works by analysing *Beauty and the Beast* and a reading of it.

This book is a distillation of my Ph.D thesis which was over 350 pages. In it two young girls aged 8 were asked to name and reconstruct their favourite fairy tale. They were then asked questions about their version of the story. The reconstruction plus associations is called the re-presentation. It is this which is analysed as another text but based in the personal circumstances of the reader and serving some idiosyncratic function for that reader.

The thesis was written as it developed; the first fairy tale's reading and analysis led onto the final model. This book, however, presents just one fairy tale, *Beauty and the Beast*, and its re-presentation by an 8-year-old girl.

1 General orientation for the reader

This book will present a coherent model to answer the question: 'What does it mean to read?' By reading I mean that process whereby an individual grasps a meaning from a text. What is postulated is an active subject who has the ability to represent his or her social world plus an active and highly structured social world that is represented.

One aspect of this social world is literature. Texts are considered to be 'high ordered' stimuli and the analysis that is contained here attempts to lay bare the conditions of meaning of texts.

The beginning of this analysis is not primarily to be found in psychology as one might have expected given the traditional obsession with the stimulus. Rather it is to be found in Poetics and Semiotics – a branch of literary criticism and a theory of language which are outside the body of traditional psychological discourse.

Reading is conceived as a clash of structures: the possible meanings of the text meet the representational processes and desires of the reader.

Two constant textual questions will be: what exactly are the conditions of meaning in a particular text and how have they structured the reader's reading? This conditioning is, it must be noted, bi-directional; the reader brings structures to the text, and consequently how the text is used, the outcome of the 'clash', is the subject matter of the book.

Texts that direct readings are intimately tied up with the socialisation of the reader. However, I am not here interested in just purely didactic messages to the child reader: didactic stories, like a lot of modern children's literature, are not fairy tales. What is interesting is how the fairy tale structures affect. In the case of the child we have a certain need or lack being brought to the structured text and the outcome is a 'lesson' of enormous importance.

I will argue that the fairy tale offers a range of meanings to the reader and that a child's favourite fairy tale is assumed to be special just because it does offer meanings that enable the reader to reduce uncertainty in its present emotional state. The text can only do that if it is itself structured around affect and if the child can identify with this structure.

We can see that this clash of structures between the growing, needing reader and the 'experienced' text must result in the production of the child in meaning: that is the child is going to be offered constellations of words to interpret emotions. However, these words will, of course, be public; they belong to codes acceptable to society, as the linguist Jakobson said: 'Private property in the sphere of language does not exist' (in Barthes, 1977, p. 21).

1.1   Methods

It seems clear that when discussing 'meaning to' a reader then traditional methods cannot help. For example, psychologists have often used 'reaction time' measures to analyse the problem of understanding thus making, as did Anderson (1976), an identity[1] between speed, intelligence and cognitive processes. This is a tragic nonsense left over from a tradition of hyper-empirical behaviourist psychology made more confusing by the use of the computer. Speed is neither intelligence nor an index of cognitive processes.

My aim is to analyse what happens when the reader is faced with a text that is relevant to her at a particular time. The method adopted is that of structuralism. Structuralism states that any activity, including reading and psychological research, functions first by decomposing the object of perception according to some rule and recomposing another object that renders the first 'intelligible'. This is accomplished by the creation of another object which 'manifests the rules of functioning of the original object' (Barthes, 1972, p. 149).

As Barthes points out:

Between the two objects ... of structuralist activity, there occurs *something new*, and what is new is nothing less than the generally intelligible: the simulacrum is intellect added to object, and this has additional anthropological value, in that it is man himself, his history, his situation, his freedom. ... (p. 150)

This methodological orientation and its reflexivity is very important. It means that the reader of the fairy tale is active in the same way as the researcher: both are creating other texts to render the original text intelligible. There is therefore a functionally equivalent set of bonds between: the reader and text; researcher and text; and the researcher and the reader's simulacrum. It follows from this that there is no real or definitive reading of text – only versions the underlying structure of which manifests certain rules of functioning.

The difference though between the reader's model and the re-

---

[1] Anderson (1976) says for example that: 'Any theory which does not ultimately address temporal features has little hope for dealing with problems of intelligence' (p. 19). By intelligence is meant representational process; quantity not quality is the goal to their understanding. 'Intelligence' is replaced here by 'intelligibility', a concept that relies on quality of 'mind' not, and it's hard to see how it could, quantity.

searcher's is that the reader's model is the result of his or her situation; while the researcher's model is the result of his situation based in the structuralist notion of science and his identification with those who do this type of research.

This is not so much a method as a theory of being; the 'addition of intellect' is, of course, the addition of language; and it is the structuralist project. It is therefore a biassed method yet so are they all, as Eco, (1977) points out:

> In the human sciences one often finds an 'ideological fallacy' common to many scientific approaches which consists in believing that one's own approach is not ideological because it succeeds in being 'objective' and 'neutral'. For my own part, I share the same sceptical opinion that all enquiry is *motivated*. Theoretical research is a form of social practice. Everyone who wants to know something wants to know it in order to do something. If he claims that he wants to know it only in order 'to know' and not in order 'to do' it means he wants to know it in order to do nothing, which is in fact a surreptitious way of doing something i.e., leaving the world just as it is (or as his approach assumes it ought to be). (Eco, 1977, p. 29)

1.2 Semiotics

The Saussurean notion of language resulted from a debate about nominalism and the place of the speaker or subject in discourse. For Saussure the place of the subject is peripheral compared with the institution of language in which each person has to be apprenticed. Language is seen as a social institution that did not 'name' objects but, as Benveniste (1971) makes clear, words or signs were in an arbitrary relationship with things and furthermore the relation between signifier and signified was simply based on 'necessary' conventions. Consequently, the meaning of things was not to be found in the things themselves (a belief held (eventually) by Bloomfield that left American linguistics sunk in syntax for a very long time) but in the system of signs itself.

This social institution is surely the greatest and most important mediator of self and object, and it becomes for Semioticians the very condition of experience.

But where is the person in all this? For Saussure the person is a mere accident, an accessory:

> In separating language (langue) from speaking (parole) we are at the same time separating:
> (1) what is social from what is individual;

(2) what is essential from what is accessory and more or less accidental. (p. 14)

'Langue' exists as a pattern over and above the person and must be referred to if individual speech acts are to be understood. It is in this sense that the subject has been displaced. No longer is the subject the source of ideas and thoughts; rather meaning moves through him. This is an important point because this book can be read as 'a search for the subject'.

Semioticians/structuralists, especially Barthes, Lévi-Strauss and more fanatically Eco, wish to dissolve the subject (which Lévi-Strauss believes to be the goal of the social sciences) who is considered to be a mere pollutant.

In one sense this follows logically from the Saussurean project but it can also be read as a reaction, almost an allergic one, to the psychologism of the individual and self that has been prevalent in literary criticism and social science for some time.

Still it is a goal of the present work not necessarily to re-centre the subject/reader but to find out what part the individual, developing, historical subject plays in the system.

The paramount system is language and it is the addition of 'intellect' to social objects that allows the structuralist to see the system. This intellect is really the wisdom found in and developed out of Saussure's *Course in General Linguistics* (1974) in which language is proposed as the source of illumination for considering other social objects and actions; once the constitutive rules of the system are 'recomposed', we then have the conditions of meaning or a system of signification. As Culler says:

> The cultural meaning of any particular act or object is
> determined by a whole system of constitutive rules: rules which
> do not regulate behaviour so much as create the possibility of
> particular forms of behaviour. (1975, p. 5)

The study of meaning or signification is uncovering these rules. For Eco (1977) as for Saussure these rules *exist*: 'When on the basis of an underlying rule, something actually presented to the perception of the addressee stands for something else, there is signification.' Codes are the rules of the system that underlie the process of communication. But for Eco human beings are only 'methodologically' necessary for getting at these rules; they actually exist over and above the person in the same way as Saussure meant that language is over and above the person.

It is a general assumption of the book that the person has two roles: he is not only the medium through which these codes are expressed but also the transformer of meaning to his or her own purpose – to match his needs.

1.3 Affect

The status of affect is extremely important, then, in the 'search for the subject' as the person reads in these systems of signification.

Meaning is always meaning *to* someone. Traditional psychology of text processing gives experimental paragraphs to subjects which have a more or less complicated syntax containing what is naively called a 'common' meaning and subjects are asked to respond YES/NO to stated inferences from these paragraphs. The speed with which they respond is then a measure of cognitive processing and a verification of their models. They miss an obvious point:

> To speak as if what is accepted and given a place in mental life is always simply a question of what fits into already formed apperception systems is to miss the *obvious* point that the process of fitting is an active process, depending directly upon the preformed tendencies and bias which the subject brings to the task. (my emphasis, Barlett, 1932, p. 85)

What would happen if the subjects of these experiments were presented with texts which were meaningful to them? Reading is always reading for some purpose or desire, and it is the articulation of desire by the tale that interests me here.

Bettelheim's (1978) idea is that fairy tales act in some way to help a child reader to sort out an 'inescapable cauldron of emotions' or inner conflict that growing up inevitably brings. If this is so then behind the text there must exist systems of signification codifying affect responses. This notion is supported by cognitive theories of emotion notably Schachter (1971) who showed that 'cognitions arising from the immediate situation as interpreted by past experience provide the framework within which one understands and labels one's emotions' (p. 5). When we put this in terms of the child's development then we can see that any framework that the child has is a received one which has been introduced to the child by society in some form.

Thus, if Saussure is right when he states that the child has to serve a linguistic apprenticeship, then reading children's fairy tales is *one* of the ways by which the child progresses to some sort of qualification. The socialisation of desire is one of the primary purposes of fairy tales. Traditionally, as M.P.M. Richards (1974) has pointed out, 'socialisation' has often been associated with neo-be-haviourism in that the person is conceived as a passive learner or trainee. Richards proposes a more active conception of the child's part in becoming a self-conscious member of society. In order to do this, 'we must also learn to see the world a little more from the child's point of view' (p. 5).

In what follows it is hoped that this goal is realised; there is no simple question of 'filling up' a passive subject because there is a dialectic interaction between reader and text where both are active for some purpose.

1.4   The text as higher ordered stimulus

In psychology the obsession with the stimulus and response pro-duced very little generally but even less on the nature of one half of the association: the stimulus.

Only J. J. Gibson (1966) gives an indication of the complexity and effect that *any* stimulus has. He pointed to three main attri-butes of the stimulus:

(1)   it always has a degree of adjacent order; form or pattern;
(2)   it always has some successive order; structure in time;
(3)   it always has some component of variance and invariance.

This information complex is 'grasped' by active perceptual sys-tems which 'hunt for clarity' but the stimulus is structured in such a way that it constrains the types of events in which it might be involved. This is his idea of affordances: objects provide informa-tion for the activities and interaction they afford.

In this book, stimuli of a high order, such as texts, afford certain interactions; they have a range of meanings. This is followed up by another idea of Gibson's which says that there are 'available' sti-muli and 'effective' stimuli. Effective ones are those that 'work' for the reader in his or her existential predicament – after all children's bookshelves are full of non-favourite (for the moment) texts.

Gibson proposes that higher ordered stimuli, although they are complex, are theoretically open to explanation and description. There is a lot in Gibson's work that recalls the structuralist way. For Gibson the main problem at the heart of the psychology of perception was not the perception of appearances or rather vari-ance but the senses' ability to perceive invariance or structure: 'The unanswered question of sense perception is how the observer ... can obtain constant perceptions in everyday life on the basis of ... changing sensations' (p. 3). This invariance is to be found in the stimulus; although it has to be grasped, its information is nevertheless 'out there'.

The connection not only with structuralism but also Saussure himself is quite clear. 'Langue' as a stimulus 'albeit of an exceptionally high order' is independent of the understanding subject and Gibson has shown that the rock bottom of language – its second level of articulation, the phoneme – is not the result of subjective perceptual processes because 'Phonemes are in the air.'

1.4.1 *Phonology to myths*

Phonology is the theory of the function of sounds in the language and it is an important part of the semiological project because of its position as the foundation of meaning as difference in the system of signs. Furthermore, this theory has been used by Lévi-Strauss (1972) in the analysis of myths which form the starting point of the text grammar presented here.

The main point about phonemes is that they are sounds which distinguish signs and thereby 'create the possibility of meaning': that is their function and the reason that they can do this has nothing to do with the subjectivity of the receiver but everything to do with the way the sound is actually produced. The very foundation for meaning is then the difference in phonemes, meaningless in themselves but the condition for meaning. Meaning is then relational not substantial, and phonemes are produced by the realisation of members of a definitive set of binary distinctive features which generates the phoneme's information.

This microscopic justification for the independence of language and its necessarily relational nature is vital because of Lévi-Strauss's use of the binary heuristic for the analysis of myths. As Jameson (1972) shows in his book, *The Prison House of Language*, Lévi-Strauss's approach to the myth is to treat it like a sign vulnerable to a structuralist analysis based on the model of the phoneme. In this analysis then the paradigmatic dimension of the 'mytheme' is 'produced' by distinctive features in the myth which only really become distinctive because of the syntagmatic relationship of the mythemes themselves. Thus, true to Saussure and Jakobson, Lévi-Strauss has to go to ever-higher levels of abstraction in order to find the difference that makes a difference between the mythemes of myth.

The ultimate 'signified' of all this, though, is not really to tell us anything at all about myths; rather it is to demonstrate a rather simple 'theory of reading'. This is that, given the binary nature of the phoneme and the binary nature of the mytheme (a unit of mythical thought), it seems reasonable that signs and myths are understood because of the brain's structured faculty to decode binary information. So because phonemes are in the air, they must be learnt by the child's brain-based ability to pick out the distinctive features of the incoming sounds. Furthermore, every culture has languages with certain sounds which are phonemic in that language. However, this occurs because what is universal here is the brain itself and the vocal apparatus for producing these phonemic sounds.

From the point of view of the hearer of the myth, it is not the person who is listening but his brain decoding unconsciously; hence the following celebrated statement: 'We do not pretend to demonstrate how men think in the myths but rather how these myths think themselves in men without them being aware of it' (in Culler, 1975, p. 50).

Myths attain to a mystical level because myths, like music, touch our innermost being; they suppress time, produce emotional *and* intellectual effects. This is especially true in the field of music where time is suppressed and another dimension can be reached.

But it is also the logical fulfilment of the semiological project; i.e., the end of the person. My wish in this book is to 'pretend' to demonstrate how men think in myths by examining how children think in fairy tales.

There is a nice irony here. One often sees a desire on the part of social scientists to 'anchor' a theory in something which is tangible, material, real. The irony is that the language is not anchored in any *thing* at all; Saussure fought that one out a long time ago. 'Langue' is a freefloating system of relations 'contingently' anchored in conventions not the brain.

For Saussure meaning is synchronic and to understand someone or some text was to have interiorised the 'langue' as it is shared at that particular moment, not as it was at another time. The current use of the 'sign' 'gay' makes this clear. Those who wish to anchor theories of social phenomena suffer the awful insecurity of no origins, one of the prime movers in producing origin myths.

The point is that by turning Lévi-Strauss upside down and by not elevating the binary method to a principle of thought (it is according to Jameson simply a stimulant to perception) then it makes sense to try this approach out on fairy tales, thereby avoiding the reductionism and re-centering the subject. The implication for a human theory of reading is that situation, motivation and biography can now be taken into account. Brains are universal; situations are not.

1.4.2   *Fairy tales*

Bettelheim's book *Tales of Enchantment* proposes that fairy tales offer solutions to the inner turmoil felt by the growing reader. But it is often unclear in his argument whether these solutions are there for the taking, a bit like a recipe, or whether they impose themselves on the 'ineffable, inarticulate, inner conflict' the reader is supposed to be going through.

In much the same way as Lévi-Strauss considers myths to be a progression of mythic thought in which contradictions are mediated, so fairy tales can be seen as progression of affective thought in which affective contradictions are mediated.

But Bettelheim shares with Lévi-Strauss a reductionist perspective in believing that sexual instinct, in the end, is that which is being mediated. Bettelheim's analyses of fairy tales only make sense within a psycho-analytic meta-psychology and with particular reference to the primary repression. Upside down Bettelheim fits into the semiological project as well. After all the child is not faced with adult readings of fairy tales; the description and understanding of how signs are concatenated in a text is not the task of psychoanalysis but that of a theory of language – or theories derived from linguistics. We need not appeal then to 'human nature'; there is no need for yet another anchor. In Bettelheim's argument emotions are 'naturalised' and, as a consequence, the fairy tale necessarily has to operate on a level that is universal: '. . . the content of the chosen tale usually has nothing to do with the reader's external life, but much to do with his inner problems, which seems incomprehensible and hence unsolvable' (p. 25).

There is no reason why anything should be tagged as universal unless it has been accepted *a priori* that this is the case or, which is more probable, the discourse within which one works forces a postulation of origination; for Lévi-Strauss this is a brain-based origin and, for Bettelheim, the psychoanalyst, an 'ultimate repression' which, it turns out, is equally biological. Both are trapped in the need for original anchors.

It follows from this that, if one accepts the biological foundations of emotional turmoil (i.e. human nature) combined with psychoanalytic meta-theory, then one has a powerful hermeneutic. Thus, Bettelheim's interpretations of particular fairy tales *are* definitive given the frame of reference he brings to the text.

1.4.3   'Thought'

If a biological anchor to affect is removed then it must be replaced by a floating theory of affect. In some way feelings that are ineffable for the child are given an externalisation by the more or less complicated affect structure of the story and the narrative patterning of the signs in it. With the erasure of ineffability comes of course the imposition of articulation; an implication of this is that emotion cannot be separated from cognition according to the proposition that, as we grow up, the ineffable is articulated for us by the cultural artefacts with which we are presented. We learn how to feel or, in another way, our feelings are cognitive. I have already quoted Bertold Brecht's remark in the introduction. As Brecht put it: 'we feel thoughtfully and we think feelingly.' Separating thought and emotion, is (to use Saussure's analogy) like trying to cut the back from the front of a piece of paper, or to use Brecht, like trying to take an adverb away from its verb. What support though, is there for the proposition that affect is an integral part of cognitive structure of the person?

Cognitive theories of emotion state that interpretations of present situations allow us to label states of feeling. What is vital to do here is to ask this question from a developmental perspective. So we can now ask: what is the process by which a feeling-state becomes an inseparable part of representational (i.e. cognitive) capacities? The assumption behind this question is that the human starts with feeling states but must, at a certain stage of development, incorporate them into a cognitive system.

If the cognitive aspect of emotion is accepted, then we can say that emotion is object-centred or 'intentional' (in the phenomenological sense); that we are always conscious of *something*. It follows from this that emotion has a purpose or a goal: emotion is a means to a particular end and, consequently, it must be explained contextually. In other words emotion is purposeful and meaningful.

One of the great cognitive tasks of the developing infant is to relate to the objects (including people) in his or her environment. Yet we could say that the neonate is faced with two primary objects right from the beginning of life, i.e. the two feeling states of well-being and discomfort. These two states of being are primary in that they precede the child's relationship with his external objects (notably the caretaking mother). It is when these objects *affect* these feeling states that the ineluctable bond between feeling state and representation develops. The most explicit and powerful explanation of this theory of affect comes in a paper by Sandler and Sandler (1978) who describe how the infant will try to maintain relations with those objects which lead to pleasure states (objects with whom interaction results in a positive feeling state) and avoid 'bad' objects (those which, during interaction, result in disturbing feelings).

Allied to this is the fact that the child will start to represent not only those objects with which he interacts but also *himself* in this interaction. Now the original goal of the interaction is to maintain the good state, a wish-fulfilment, that, thanks to human cognition, can now be carried out in fantasy, dreams, day dreams as well as in reality. The actual form of these relationships will depend upon the particular circumstances of the child as he or she develops; they will nevertheless become structured over the years as they are efficacious in maximising the once good feeling-state:

> In the development of the object relationship (i.e. structured role relationships) the part played by affective experience is central. An experience only has or retains meaning for a child *if it is linked with feeling*. The assumption is made that ultimately all meaning is developmentally functionally related to states of feeling. (Sandler and Sandler 1978, p. 292) (my emphasis)

Only with the development of representational processes and self and other, does the child attempt, through previously learnt role relationships with its mother, to reinstate the constellation of pleasurable feelings which, because of the increasing boundary between self and other, the child can no longer assume to be forthcoming. The complications of human inter-subjectivity arise when one tries to reinstate good feelings through manipulating the other into a role relationship that is, and has always been, efficacious in doing this for us. So, as we develop, various strategies of relating arise which are ways of obtaining some sort of affirmation of security, a general term used by Sandler and Sandler (1978) for the constellation of good affect that adults try for:

> The urge to re-experience important subjective aspects of object relationships from the first years of life constantly recurs and persists ... particularly when our feelings of security or safety are threatened as they constantly are. (p. 287)

Here affect itself is incorporated into the child's representations of his objective world and thereby becomes a privileged, but not separate, part of his conscious and unconscious mental apparatus.

It also follows from this that affect is social. It may be particular to the family context but it nevertheless is an act of sociality in that the 'objects' of the child's life are as significant as the self: 'the object plays as important a role as the self in the mental representations which is part of the wish' (p. 291). The advantage of adopting this perspective is that it allows one to think about affect not as ontologically apart from thought but rather as *part* of thought.

Also, just as there is no 'private' language, there is no private emotion, for emotion is always a *relation*. Emotions are possible because of other people in much the same way that language is possible and necessary because of other people.

1.4.4   *The structure of the text: Propp, Greimas and the case grammar*

We can now ask what is it about the system of significations in the text that create the possibility of coherent, accepted emotions for the child reader. Given the Sandlers' formulation and our release from the twin anchors of binary decoding brain matter and sexual instinct, we can begin to uncover this 'allowing' structure of the text.

At one level then it will have a binary structure called the affect signified. But although this is adequate for the affect structure of the text, it tells us very little about the 'narrative' patterning of the signs and the tales' specific 'literanoust', to use a term from the Russian formalists such as Propp to denote literariness.

It is in fact to the formalist Propp (1968) that we should look for guidance here. He was able to show that plots of folk tales are dependent upon abstract formal relations referring to actions and functions rather than, as was the previous method of categorisation, type of character: these invariant functions are what give folk tales their literariness. For example, an ogre in one tale could be replaced by a dragon or a troll in another tale; content is dependent upon the place or origin of the story – Russian, German, etc. The plot, however, is dependent upon more abstract, formal relationships which refer to actions and functions rather than to type of character. Propp's (1968) point is that this is the feature that makes folk tales a literary fact; they remain constant with variable content:

The characters' actions represent constants while everything else can vary. For example:

(1)   The king sends Ivan to find the princess. Ivan leaves.
(2)   The king sends Ivan to find a rare object. Ivan leaves, etc.

... and so on. The sending on the search, and the departure,
are constants. The sender and the leaver, the motivation for the
sending are variables. (In Miranda, 1972, p. 139).

Once again as with the structuralist analysis, the emphasis is upon
the invariants. For Propp these invariants are of essentially two
types:

(i)   the role, that may take a variety of characters given the venue
in which the tale originates, and
(ii)   the function, which is a particular action that is significant as
it relates the whole story or plot.

But being a formalist, Propp (1968) did not stop at the original
corpus upon which he developed these ideas (i.e. Russian fairy
tales); he tried, instead, to incorporate them into a universal grid
of fairy tale roles and functions:

The researcher can prove that different tales, such as the
Egyptian tale of two brothers, the tale of the firebird, the tale
of the Morozok, the tales of the fisherman and the fish as well
as a number of myths, justify joint study. (p. 140)

He attempted this by isolating a set of 150 roles and a set of 31
functions. Thus, for example, X gives Y a horse contains one function 'giving' and 3 elements or roles. X becomes the 'benefactor',
Y is the 'receiver', 'horse' is the object given. He made a grid of
roles and functions into which all fairy tales can be put; those that
cannot do not qualify as fairy tales. 'Conversely, every tale that
could be entered on the chart is a fairy tale and every one that
cannot belongs to another type of tale' (p. 140). This is a good
example of 'early' structuralism employing a deep structure 'generating machine' (the grid) that produces all fairy tales and no non-
fairy tales. This analysis suffers like all such systems from the lack
of an understanding of content vis-à-vis the important and related
question of reading. Nevertheless, the analysis of underlying structure that Propp initiated was taken up by Greimas in a fruitful
way.

1.4.5   *Greimas's development of Propp's structure*

What Propp considers to be a function of plot, Greimas considers to be a function of words themselves.[2] It is not the individual word that Greimas thinks important but rather the 'dramatic structure' which he points out exists and is common to *ALL* types of discourse. That is to say, he maintains that words enter into *relationships* with each other, or play roles vis-à-vis each other. The failure of Lévi-Strauss's method for the narative fairy tale is that it sees the tales as a single signifier rather than as a linear complex series of signs – the basic structure of which is dramatic: 'If we recall that *functions* in traditional syntax are but roles played by words – the subject being "the one who performs the action", the object "the one who suffers it, etc." (in Culler, 1975, p. 124). Thus the spectacle or play the words act out is: 'unique in that it is permanent: the content of the actions changes all the time, the actors vary, but the enunciation spectacle remains forever the same, for its permanence is guaranteed by the fixed distribution of the basic roles' (p. 124).

The invariance (permanence) here is the *sentence* seen as a predicate with a constellation of roles. Greimas conceives of six different roles: subject, object, sender, receiver, opponent and helper; there are two types of predicate: the function, sometimes called the dynamic predicator and qualifications called static predicates. In addition, a predicate may also include an adverbial element called an aspect.

Here, Greimas demonstrates that what Propp was talking about can be handled as well in linguistic terms. But Propp also has the advantage of allowing us to say how sentences are related to one another, i.e. how the text is structured, whereas Greimas' analysis leaves us at the *sentence's* dramatic structure. So, for Propp, functions are not simply actions or predicates in *a* sentence; they also get a meaning from their role in the story as a whole. As Culler (1975) points out, this is necessary and something that Greimas misses: 'he (Greimas) gives no indication as to how his model would deal with all the problems of the relationship between sentences...' (p. 83).

So a combination of Propp's and Greimas's ideas might produce the foundation for an answer to a major problem of textual structures, i.e. the need for an adequate sentential analysis that informs

---

[2] One can see here the radical difference between formalism and structuralism. The former concentrated upon the 'literary fact' while the latter, because of Saussure, concentrated upon the work's linguistic nature.

also about the macro structure of the text. What remains is a method for doing this.

The path from Propp to Greimas reveals that what is thought to be invariant is analogous to 'case grammar' which also talks about predicates and their roles but conceived as grammatical cases. Moreover, case grammar can provide both a method and notation that incorporates what is useful in Propp and Greimas and, at the same time, advances the theoretical understanding of both text and reading.

1.4.6 *Case grammar*

This is the term given to the 'logical' relations that exist between nouns and between nouns and verbs in sentences. Although Fillmore (1968) claimed they:

> comprise a set of universal, presumably innate, concepts which identify certain types of judgement, human beings are capable of making about the events that are going on about them, judgements about such matters as who did it, who it happened to and what got changed. (p. 1)

No such assumption about universality of concepts is made here; rather the assumption is made, along with Piaget (1971), that concepts, even that of object constancy, have to be learned through a process of activity or construction.

The use of case grammar here is to make the needed link between signs and sentential meaning, and from there the problem of the higher order structure, the text, can be resolved.

1.4.7 *Case grammar and the structure of the text*

What follows is a rather skeletal idea of the text as a higher ordered stimulus which will be 'fleshed out' in Part II.

1.4.7.1 *Affect signified*

Although the case grammar is vital in revealing levels of structure it is really at the level of affect that the decomposition has to start; after all it is assumed here that fairy tales are structured around affect.

The method then is to identify affectemes or affect signifieds in the text which are clearly delimited by a set of sentences. This set in turn becomes a Signifying Unit which is a unit of reading.

Methodologically, an SU gets its status *as* an SU because it signifies a particular affect. Although the initial decomposition is centered around the affect-signified this does not mean that the final differentiation is decided upon because of the affect. It is the function of the case analysis to reveal the dramatic structure which allows one to ascertain the real basis for difference. In most cases, it will be seen that an SU gets its status because of the affect that it signifies; on the other hand there are certain points in the narrative, in Part II, where affect does not have such a privileged place as differentiator (see SUs 18 and 19). The affect signified remains, however, the original, intuitively based access into the test's structure; the case analysis clarifies the intuition.

These sets of sentences are then broken down, stopped and translated by the case analysis, and I would like to argue that the case proposition leads to a fuller understanding of what the child reader is faced with. This is accomplished through an analysis that reveals the 'dramatic' structure of the text (Greimas and Propp) by a decomposition that stays at the level of signification. Studies in comprehension will not succeed by a *theoretical* reduction to 'innate categories' (cf. Fillmore, 1968) or a methodological reduction to 'temporal features' (cf. Anderson (1976) and Kintsch (1974)).

Case propositions represent a language for systematising the inter-relationships of words: it is another 'stimulant for perception' to understand a sentence and, as will be shown, large groups of *connected* sentences, i.e. a text. The 'intermediate' decomposition so effected has certain effects:

(i) The text is made to 'slow down'. It is one of the most important methodological axioms of cognitive psychology that the object of study is cognised too quickly for adequate analysis; cognitive processes are fast. In the past the object of study was slowed down to assess the cognitive process by using relatively simple 'story paragraphs' which contained a rather torpid logical structure to which inferences of a Yes/No type were made. The slowing down that the decomposition allows is one that will actually tell us about the action of the object of cognition as well as the act of cognition. It will allow the full complexity of a 'naturally' occurring cultural artefact (i.e. a fairy tale as opposed to an artificial paragraph in an experiment in cognitive psychology) written for reasons that must lie outside 'experimental' psychology.

(ii) The decomposition proposed will provide a notation that, in a real sense, structures the text for the researcher.

In 1972 Lindsay and Norman published *Human Information Processing: Introduction to Psychology*, in which they created a notation using case grammar to represent an event as a series of propositions interconnected and held together by 'case' vectors. Thus, the simple proposition: FATHER loves BEAUTY is represented like this:

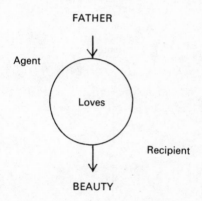

Figure 1.1   Case proposition

Where the circle is the verb or *predicator*; Father is the agent of the verb and Beauty is the recipient of the action. The arrows are the vectors. Also the nouns in question can be elaborated if needed by attributes which are connected by lines, so:

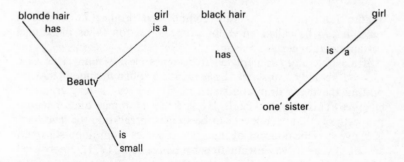

Figure 1.2   Attributes

However, for an event a way is needed of expanding propositions. To this end the authors provide the 'purpose' case vector; so for the proposition: THE FATHER went yesterday to the SHIP to see the CAPTAIN:

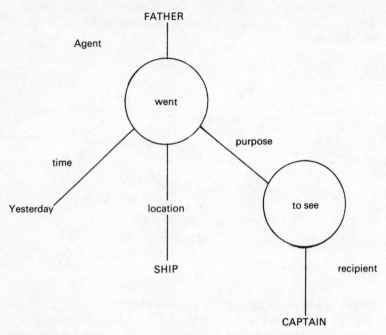

Figure 1.3   A 'case event'

Figure 1.3 represents a more complicated proposition and in a sense it can be called an event where an action takes place at a certain time for certain reason.

If a whole story is depicted it becomes clear visually (the case method actually translates the text into a different mode) that by putting the text's dramatic structure in this way a text grammar emerges. This reveals a multi-levelled text grammar one of whose properties is that each level can be seen as integrating the level that is above it. This concept of integration comes from linguistics and specifically as it was formulated by Benveniste (1971). Each level of language integrates the next higher level in the sense that the lower unit enters and completes the higher level. The *meaning* of a unit is its capacity to integrate higher units. The *form* of a unit is its composition in terms of lower level units.

Starting at the lowest level we find the dramatically tagged signifiers.

1.4.7.2 *Level of signifiers*

Propositions are integrated by signifiers. It is clear that we cannot know in advance what will or will not constitute a primary signifier for the reader. However, within the text itself there will be signifiers which are vital in two ways:

(i) those signifiers that are important to the structure of the narrative, that allow it to be a narrative, I shall call 'key' signifiers;
(ii) those that are important for the highest level of signification to be discussed below I shall call 'primary'.

Key signifiers will receive a (+) notation and primary signifiers will receive a (*) notation. All signifiers will get a case value attached to them. Although the intermediate case analysis of section 1.4.7 remains intact there are certain changes and conventions that the reader will have to know about. Here are some of the conventions.

(i) Verbs are grouped at the end of the list of signifiers and it is this grouping that gives the clue to the type of dramatic structure of the SU. Each verb has attached to it its adverb.
(ii) Verb forms whose infinitives are 'to be' or 'to have' have been left out. This is for economy of presentation and also because the concepts of 'being' and 'having' are relatively self-evident from the cases that signifiers take around them. To this end the case of a person who 'has' or 'is' I have labelled agent (A); I am aware that this raises philosophical problems: 'Is one the agent of one's being?' etc. I simply make the assumption that this is so. Furthermore, this is also my stance for emotions: if you become angry, I label 'you' to be the agent.
(iii) The case notion of possession is handled by attribute (att).
(iv) Prepositions are kept with their verbs. A further, more atomistic decomposition would take me beyond that which we need to know in order to read the story. To this end conditional 'if ... then' type SU's have received a translation, see SU8, for example.
(v) There is a new case of comparison (comp) found at SU 24. This arises because it contains a simile that is dramatically important.

For the most part a description of the signifiers is redundant, but where necessary I will point out the importance of a particular case value.

1.4.7.3   *The level of the proposition*

Signifiers integrate the proposition. A proposition is defined by its dramatic structure as revealed by the case analysis. For the analysis a proposition simply *has to be*; it is the ultimate foundation for any signification at all. We can ascertain 5 types of dramatic structure categorised at this level:

(i)   Descriptive: where a scene or situation is described.

(ii)   Factual: where an action or series of actions are stated for the reader's information.

(iii)   Action: where an episode in the story takes place.

(iv)   Anticipatory: where action is anticipated.

(v)   Conditional: where a character sets conditions.

1.4.7.4   *Level of results*

Propositions result in other propositions. So propositions integrate the next level called the 'results' level. I will show that this is a vital part of the grammar because it is the basis for the coherence of the story. Because of this it is that level of the text where an important interface with the reader takes place. Here, I hope to show that the results level not only obeys the recomposition rule of integration but that it also has a privileged place in relation to the 'socialising' level of signification. The model to be presented demonstrates that the 'results' section can be categorised in such a way as to indicate clearly how this important level functions both in the text and in the process of reading. The model uncovers an important binary classification which gives to the results section its important function vis-à-vis the reader – the structure of the text and the structure of language.

The two classifications are:

(1)   Internal results

These are propositions or parts of propositions whose coherence relies on something that has already taken place in the text. If we are told, for example, a character in a story is 'stupid' and some time later he is involved in a stupid action, then the action is coherent given the previous proposition.

(2)   External results

These are propositions whose coherence is given by the experience of the reader. The reader is asked to fill in the gap in intelligibility that the text has not answered or has not as yet answered.

In theory, internal results can have 5 modes of operation:

(i)   repetition: where an identical action happens at two points in the story.
(ii)   similarity: where actions are linked by a particular theme they have in common. This theme will refer to another level, usually the affect signified, in the model.
(iii)   inversion: where coherence owes its existence to an inverted action that happened previously.
(iv)   completion: where an earlier, unfinished action is completed later on.
(v)   factual: an action can receive coherence because of facts stated earlier in the text.

Two external results can have three modes of operation.

(i)   inter-textual: where a proposition is coherent because of other stories. (In this sense the structuralist would say that the text is a network of other texts, cf. Figure, 1.5, p. 41.)
(ii)   the 'natural': these propositions are coherent because of 'scientific beliefs' about the natural world – what goes up must come down.
(iii)   the cultural: where the reader is referred to 'ways of doing' in his/her environment; facts of the cultural world.

From the point of view of the reading, external results require more effort than internal results which only require a memory of the previous propositions in the story.

Internal results operate upon a horizontal dimension: they are contiguously related on a dimension that linguists would call the syntagmatic. External results operate upon a vertical dimension. The reader is asked to look for *similar* examples in his/her experience. This is what the linguist would call the paradigmatic dimension.

It is here at the level of the external result that tearing the text away from its reception is most difficult; can the text exist in the absence of a reading? I hope to show from *my* reading that, although this level is an important interface between reader and text and thus vital to the process of reading, it is also something that exists in the text itself before its reception.

The next level is that of grammatical units. There are five of these in the model and they serve various functions which will become clear in Part II.

1   Transitions, generally for moving the story along.

2   The Introduction which is a type of transition involving a sus-
pension of reality testing.
3   Episodes, which are marked by an internal structure.
4   Events, which are 'all of a piece'.
5   An Ending which is a type of event.

Although the case analysis reveals the structure of the text it
does not tell us anything about the text's relationship to the
'langue' or systems of communication. Furthermore, although it
plays a part in communicating with the reader, it is only part of
the story as to how the texts get opposite messages across to the
reader.

This is accomplished by the last level of the text.

1.4.7.5   *The level of semiosis: the S-level*

By semiosis I mean that meanings are articulated for the reader,
are offered to the reader as *possible*, to a greater or lesser extent,
constructions of reality. Semiosis is then opposed to mimesis; it is
not an imitation of the reader's world but a particular set of articulations of it.

In this section I want to explain the sixth level of the model
because it is new to the argument presented so far. I will rely very
much upon the theories of such semioticians as Barthes (1977) and
Eco (1977). My main aim will be to demonstrate how it is possible
for the fairy tale to constitute a reader's feelings; how in fact the
child reader comes to articulate the ineffable through reading the
story.

This level invites the reader to *think* about what is happening in
the story and his/her life. Although it is obviously necessary to
consider this function as it is organised in the text itself, I will
attempt to give a foundation for it taken from semiotics and then
re-insert this argument back into the model when the actual text is
analysed.

1.4.7.6   *Semiotics: the sign, message, code and signification*

It will be recalled that semiotics is concerned first and foremost
with the nature of the linguistic sign. This is because, although its
subject matter can be any system of communication based upon
convention, the linguistic system is the 'paradigm' system. For
Saussure, the sign is an arbitrary relationship between the signifier
and the signified.

The meaning of a sign is twofold:

(i) its *signification*, the act of correlating the signifier with the signified, and
(ii) its *value* vis-à-vis the other signs that form its context in the 'langue'.

I mentioned above that researchers took either one of two aspects of the sign into their work; they either studied the organisation of the signifier or the organisation of the signified.

The study of the organisation of the signifier is more accessible than the study of the signified because of its materiality; the linguistic spoken sign has 'sonority'. I have shown, however, what the outcome of this was: a universal signified.[3]

The study of the organisation of the content on the other hand presents logical problems from the outset. One cannot isolate the content because it needs a signifying system to get round in; it needs a material vehicle.[4]

For Roland Barthes (1973), before speech the signified is nothing more than 'an undefined mass of concepts which could be compared to a huge jelly fish, with uncertain articulations and contours' (p. 118). It seems clear that the 'act' or 'process' whereby the signifier is correlated with the signified, i.e. the signification, is the area where *semiotic research* will be fruitful. It must be remembered, however, that for semioticians at least, this 'act' or 'process' mentioned above does not mean any 'psychologism'. The human being is simply the methodologically necessary element for a semiotics; theoretically the 'langue' provides meaning. As soon as an act of speech is perceived as a communication, '... it is already part of the "langue", and ... to separate the "langue" from speech means ipso facto constituting the problematics of meaning' (Barthes, 1977, pp. 16-17).

Because they are interested in communication systems, semioticians find a communications theory framework useful. The most important use is the identification of code/message with langue/parole. This identification happens for the following reasons:

The first reason stems from the work of Benveniste (1971) who

---

[3] According to Hjelmslev (1961), Saussure must have realised that artificial separation of the expression from the content was meaningless (p. 50).

[4] This is also prefigured in Saussure and best brought out by Lacan (1966) who shows that the signified 'slides under' the signifier in that we can never grasp it as 'pure' thought but only through the relationship of signifiers, what he calls the chain of signifiers; an idea which the level of signifiers in the model attempts to encapsulate.

shows that what *is* arbitrary about the sign is its relationship to the *referent*, the thing in the world. On the other hand, the relationship between the signifier and the signified is said to be necessary; no English speaker has the right to alter these connections in the 'langue' and they are in this sense necessary.[5]

A code is a convention or a rule which correlates the two aspects of the sign in the actual message. They are, therefore, necessary in the sense that Benveniste means.

The second reason follows partly from the first: without the notion of a coded message, we are unable to account for the fact that the 'langue' taken as a whole contains several discourses, such as the culinary, fashion, scientific, etc., which, though they may overlap, for the most part can be said to have 'areas' of the 'langue' to themselves. The notion of 'langue' is much too amorphous to account for this fact. 'Code' on the other hand gives us the notion of several codes, perhaps overlapping, which organise explicit messages in different discourses.

The third reason is that, for semioticians, a code guarantees comprehension outside the person, fixed as it is in an explicit rule which generates the message. A cumbersome subjective infinite regression is, therefore, removed from the field of study – the subject only being a methodological necessity. A 'pure' and contemporary statement of this position concerning the code comes from Umberto Eco (1977).

For Eco what correlates the expression (signifier) and the content (signified) is the code. The code apportions the one to the other and the result is not so much a sign but (after Hjelmslev) a sign function:

> A sign function is realised when two functives (expression and content) enter into a mutual correlation; the same function can also enter into another correlation, thus becoming a different functive and, therefore, giving rise to a new sign function. Thus, signs are the provisional result of coding rules which establish *transitory* correlations of elements, each of these elements being entitled to enter – under given coded circumstances – into another correlation and thus form a new sign. (p. 49)

In other words the correlation of expression to content is regulated by given codes; they are what makes sign functions possible. Thus,

---

[5] 'Saussure says that "a language is always a legacy" and that consequently it is, as it were, naturalised' (in Barthes, 1977, p. 51).

'a message is nothing more than such a correspondence realised during a transmission process' (p. 54).

The next reason for the identification of langue/parole and code/ message is similar in theme to the other two. Saussure (1974) real- ised, but could not account for, the fact that within the 'langue' there were already forms 'fixed syntagms' such as compound words or strings such as the French 's'il vous plait'. In other words, the distinction upon which semiology was to be built, i.e. langue/par- ole, was blurred by the concept of 'fixed syntagms', 'There is prob- ably also a whole series of sentences which belong to the language, and which the individual no longer has to combine himself' (Saus- sure, 1974, p. 19). Barthes calls these 'stereotypes' and the notion of code here, as an explicit rule sanctioning the function, allows semiotics to accept and account for a 'langue' which is more and more 'necessary'.

The final reason is directly related to the practice of semiotics. The idea of a code now allows researchers to concentrate upon the last area of work foreshadowed by Saussure's re-thinking of the sign, that of the process of signification itself. This is that process of the correlation of the expression and the content, the production of a sign function which is made possible by the code. For Eco, then, a code is 'a system of signification', and the process of signi- fication depends upon this system. The actual occurrence of the sign function is a communication with an interpreting human re- ceiving a message.

1.4.7.7 *Connotation and denotation*

So far I have only talked about the part of the meaning of a sign (now a sign function) conceived of by semioticians as the signifi- cation. The other side to the sign's meaning is that of value. It will be recalled that, for Saussure, there are only negative values in the language; the meaning of a sign is its difference in the system of signs which is the 'langue'. It has already been pointed out, how- ever, that already in the 'langue' there are fixed syntagms. These are concatenations of signs whose organisation is imposed upon the speaker because of a code; 'thank you very much indeed' is a combination of signs whose meaning has been generated by the courtesy code of English. In a similar vein, 'yours faithfully' at the end of a letter receives its meaning from the letter writing code of English when the name of the addressee is not referred to at the beginning.

If these syntagms were taken at the level of the individual sign they would produce some odd interpretations ('I remain, sir, your humble and obedient servant, etc.,' taken from past manifestations of the code makes this rather more clear) and they are really only meaningful as 'texts', already written for the speaker, whose meaning is at a level of signification different from that of the individual signs.

In order to capture this, linguists see two levels of signification: the denotative, the level of the self-contained individual sign and the connotative, a level which uses the first level to convey another meaning.

Eco (1977) says: 'There is a connotative semiotics when there is semiotics whose expression plane is another semiotics' (p. 55). At the level of the individual sign, the meaning of 'rose' as a bush and a sign of passion 'passionified roses' (according to Barthes, 1972, p. 113) is the difference between denotation and connotation. The following figure makes this clear.

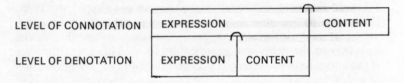

Figure 1.4   The form of the semiotics of denotation and connotation
⋂ = *existence of a code*

Figure 1.4 shows that, at the denotative level, a particular expression is correlated with a particular content; in the above example we have the expression 'rose' correlated with the content or signified *rose*. When, however, I take roses to my mistress, what was a sign function on the denotative level becomes, on the connotative level, the expression for another content; in Eco's terms there is another sign function and, therefore, another code. This seems reasonable; there is a code in our society at the present time that sanctions the giving of roses to 'female loved-ones' as a message of one's passion, the roses stand for something else to someone.

This, however, leads to an interesting and continual debate in the semiotics of denotation and connotation. Can there *ever* be a denotative semiotics in the sense that 'rose' means a particular thing. This notion of a 'referential' denotation is supported by Barthes (1973) but is contradicted by Eco (1977):

> ... even when the referent could be the object named or
> designated by the expression, when language is used in order to
> mention something, one must nonetheless maintain that an
> expression does not, in principle, designate any object, but on
> the contrary *conveys a cultural content*. (p. 61)

In the example of the 'rose' what is denoted is what we in our culture define as a rose (thing). It seems clear that the signification here is sanctioned by a code which we could call the botanical or horticultural. The meaning of rose has nothing to do with the bush but everything to do with the cultural content or unit that is correlated, through a code, with an expression. 'Every attempt to establish what the referent of a sign is forces us to define the referent in terms of an abstract entity which moreover is only a cultural convention' (p. 66).[6]

The same applies to the sign-function 'passionified roses'. Although the meaning is found at the connotative level of signification, it is nonetheless organised by a code or system of signification. The example of the rose allows another point to be made, namely that both significations depend upon codes which can be said to be very *stable* in our society. This is a very important point. The sign at the denotative level is not significant because it refers to some object but because of a stable code that correlates expresion with content. On the other hand can we say the same about the connotative level? According to Barthes (1973) this is impossible; meanings which we consider to be connotative must be understood because of a vaguer, more woolly, code: 'As for the signified of connotation, its character is at once general, global, and diffuse: it is if you like a fragment of ideology ... we might say that ideology is the form ... of the signifieds of connotation' (pp. 91-2).

In *Mythologies* (1973) Barthes is looking for an analysis of the signified (content). The logical problem here is that a signified needs a signifier. Barthes's (1973) method of getting round this is brilliant but, unfortunately, idiosyncratic. He invents words. New signs are meant to signify 'general, global and diffuse' contents,

---

[6] I am aware that this is not simply a modern semiotic debating point but that it also forms part of the history of philosophy concerned with meaning; the terms used there are extensional and intensional semantics. The first is concerned with the conditions of truth of a particular proposition and the latter with conditions of signification. It should be clear that the notion of codes is caught up with signification, as Eco (1977) says:

> Within the framework of a theory of codes it is unnecessary to the notion of extension, nor to that of possible worlds; the codes, insofar as they are accepted by a society, set up a cultural world which is neither actual nor possible in the ontological sense; its existence is linked to a cultural order, which is the way in which a society thinks ... (p. 61)

pieces of ideology:

> China is one thing, the idea which a French petty bourgeois
> not so long ago had about it is something else again: there can
> be no other name, for this characteristic mixture of little bells,
> rickshaws and opium dens, than that of *sinity*. (p. 79).

For Barthes the use of the neologism 'captures' this vague ideological concept or content that the French have of China. But captures
from whom? For Barthes and fellow semioticians *sinity* may capture what the ideology of French petty bourgeois is, but is that
how the petty bourgeois himself actually goes about interpreting
'bells, rickshaws and opium dens'? The point here is that the inven-
tion of *sinity* is a meta-language, also outlined by Hjelmslev (1961)
in that the plane of the first level of signification (denotation) becomes the content for the expression (in this case 'sinity'); meta-
language is the inversion of connotation.

I am concerned with the process whereby connotative messages are
conveyed to an interpreting human addressee. In the example of the
rose there seems no doubt that both levels of signification are based
upon codes and that both codes are stable in society at the present
time. Those codes which underlie, as systems of signification, connotative messages Eco calls sub-codes; our passion is regulated by the
sub-code which sanctions, in context, the bringing of roses to lovers.

The important, and essentially Saussurean, point being made
here is that these codes or sub-codes *exist*; rules relating expression
to content in our society at a particular time exist.

This may be true for the single sign of the rose. One could
reasonably ask how connotation handles syntagms. I mentioned
above how certain sentences already exist in the language and that
these must be referred to a code for interpretation. This is the
question of value and I showed that the differentiation posed by
Saussure was 'necessary'. However, by the same token, it is not
only the single sign that can be used at the connotative level.
'Several denoted signs can be grouped together to form a single
connotor' (Barthes, 1973, p. 91). (A connotor is the expression
rectangle on the connotation plane of signification in Figure 1.4.)

In this way, for example, a single experiment in reinforcement
learning can signify behaviorism at the connotative level. But this
level can also be elevated to signify another content, let us say,
'empirical psychology'. It can be seen that someone could go on
elevating from here to all sorts of connotative content.

With the introduction of 'someone' interpreting – getting the
message – the problem of infinite regression emerges; after all, what
is there to stop an endless elevation? Stated another way, what is
the relationship between the codes of the language and thought?

Eco (1977) takes the view that there is a process of, what he calls, unlimited semiosis – infinite regression – the human subject simply being a methodological tool to demonstrate this.

Two points can be made here in favour of the subject as *theoretically* necessary as well. In the first place, although codes are external to the human subject, they are also created by human subjects. It seems certain that any diachronic analysis of codes has to take people into account theoretically; it is only to the extent that there *are* other people that codes exist. The second point is that the use to which codes are put is also more than a mere methodological event, it has real theoretical importance for the study of reading. Codes, I will argue, constrain the regression by directing readers through particular chains of association. Moreover, there are other constraints in the process of reading, all of which I will explore below.

I began this further discussion of semiotics with the question of the meaning of a sign being its signification and value within the system of signs called the 'langue'. Semioticians study systems of communication based upon convention, and they have tried to use the distinction code/message for several reasons. I think that this identification of langue/parole *is* useful, but, like 'langue', code has been elevated to being an *independent* semiotic construct. They seem to be falling into the same irrelevance as theories of linguistic *competence* have done. It can only be made relevant by the positioning of the human addressee/addressor into the discourse of the code as a creator and user of it.

1.4.7.8   *Constraints on infinite regression*

There are two major constraints upon the interpreter of the message: one is the text within which the code is situated and the other is the desire of the reader, his/her interests, the reason why this is her favourite fairy tale.

I intend to show below that the reader will be invited to think about codes in either of two ways. In the first place, the code will be familiar and used in an accepted manner; in the second, codes will be presented which, because of their position in the story, could be used to make sense out of certain situations both in the text and in the life of the reader. Generally, there will be an invitation to think about the code, the outcome of which will depend upon the relative stability of the code, its structure in the text, the thought structure of the reader and his/her desires.

It is at the last level of the text – the S level – where I hope to be able to show these ideas clearly; its function is not to imitate the child's world but to articulate it for her, leading her to possible interpretations of her feelings. Codes are, however, external and social and it is in this sense that I see the text as a conspiracy: it allows the reader to think about her feelings in a coded, accepted and social way.

1.4.7.9   *Some definitions in summary*
The reader will need some definitions to understand what follows.

(1)   Systems of signification: this refers to the code and exists, as Eco says: 'when there is a socially conventionalised possibility of generating sign-functions'. The Saussurean question of value is contained here because it does not matter whether or not these social conventions correlate one functive (expression) to another functive (content) or if one functive happens to be a whole text which is correlated to, say, a single functive so long as there is a social convention sanctioning the correlation.

(2)   Process of signification: there is a process of signification when the system of signification allows a sign-function in actual discourse; furthermore, this process of signification must have at least one interpreting human subject. There is a process of signification when someone reads a text, i.e. when the sign functions arouse an interpretive process in the human reader. According to Hjelmslev: 'A priori it would seem to be a generally valid thesis that for every *process* there is a corresponding *system.* ....' In other words there can be no process of signification without the underlying system of signification but, from the preceding discussion, within the development of the human there can be no system without the process.

Before the analysis in Part II begins, I will list below some of the important codes that the text draws on in the *Beauty and the Beast*.

(1)   An important code is 'the problem-to-be-solved code'. This holds out the promise that if one reads on there will be more information leading to a resolution. Barthes termed this the hermeneutic code, and it is based upon the logic of puzzle/solution; question/answer found in the novel. Barthes's code is a way of organising events in a text which are based upon one's experience of other texts and the world; questions are posed and solutions promised, hence the continual participation of the reader. For Barthes: 'The units (that belongs to the code) are so many flashes of that something that has been *already* read, seen, done, lived: the code is the wake of the already. .... A code is one of the voices of which the text is woven.'

There is a lot here that is similar to my version of codes, but it does not account for the process of setting the codes up – the child reader may not have *already* seen, done, or not yet 'fixed' the already. In addition, his idea of hermeneusis reconstitutes a division between affect and cognition which is no longer tenable; these problems are *felt* by the child. The question/answer idea seems primarily cognitive, and we must remember that the 'hermeneutic code' was constructed by Barthes around an adult's reading of an adult short story.

It seems better to me to construct this code around the problem-solving experience that the child already has lived; the ability to answer questions and, what is more important, the ability to recognise questions and problems that need, for whatever reason, to be solved. It is safe to do this when dealing with child readers because this is certainly a 'wake' in which they are well established. If I am to stick to the project of describing what the child is faced with, then it seems clear she is faced with problems to be solved, internally and externally.

Barthes's notion that what the reader is faced with is a voice has a somewhat mystical feeling to it and the distinction between text and reader disappears with it. Indeed, from the semiotician's point of view the disappearance of the reader is not such a great loss to social science anyway. However, the idea that what the reader is faced with are problems that are resolvable, through thinking about them, brings the reader back into the situation. I think that this alone would justify my use of the problem-to-be-solved code.

(2)   Another code is the father/daughter which associates the vital attributes that daughter and father share: love, affection, caring, and worrying about the other.
(3)   Another code is the responsibility code which revolves around the notion of not harming or bringing harm to other human beings.
(4)   The fairy tale code is constantly used to inform the reader's reading.

This last code brings up an interesting point about codes and that is their stability. Stable codes are those which label all the key attributes that are subsumed in the code complex. Thus daughter/father shares loving, kindness, etc. A code which is unstable in our society is one where the metaphors are unlabelled, where only some key attributes are shared.

In Part II I will show how the text draws on each of these codes; I will also show it sets up codes as possible ways of thinking about problems and how this is related to the problem-to-be-solved code.

1.5   Reading and the text

So far most of the space has been given to the higher ordered stimulus called the text. Reading here is defined as investing meaning within the systems of signification of the text for some purpose. This depends upon two processes:

1.5.1   *Identification and projection*[7]

One of the main ways the child contacts the text is by these two processes.

Bettelheim (1978) points out that fairy tales are marked by the fact that the characters in them are, usually, unnamed. This is no accident. In his section on the comparison of myths and fairy tales, he shows that the function of namelessness in the fairy tale is part of their ability to 'subtly suggest solutions to inner conflict' by allowing the reader into the story via the mechanisms of identification and projection.

By presenting the child with 'generic' characters the tale does not run the risk of isolating the reader's emotional tie: 'Even when the hero is given a name, as in the Jack stories, or in "Hansel and Gretel", the use of very common names makes them generic terms, standing for any boy or girl' (p. 40). Mythical heros, he points out, are named and, being named, are felt by the reader to be alien to them. Their literary function is to maintain the myth on epic and heroic dimensions – something no child could identify with or project his emotions into; the point is that naming is a device that permits superhuman action that is carried out by an impossible 'other'. The use of 'boy' or 'girl', however, is a device that permits 'ordinary' problems to be presented and worked out by anyone.

The general proposition seems correct; that is that *one* of the devices that allows the fairy tale genre to exist is the generic naming. 'Girl' could be the reader and this depends on the character's place in the story and that story's relevance to the reader. Identification and projection are considered to be axioms underpinning the active nature of reading. From my point of view, however, projection and identification do not take place with just 'any' girl

---

[7] The term 'projective identification' could be used here, meaning an attribution to the other person or that person's situation of certain traits of the self, or even an overall resemblance of one's self but it has been too closely associated with Klien's use of the term which emphasises its importance as 'a particular form of identification which establishes the prototype of an aggressive object-relation' (Laplanche, J. and Pontalis, J.-B., 1973, p. 356).

character in any story, but with the girl character who has specific attributes in a situation whose structure and content are relevant to the reader. Important signifiers such as 'girl' have a central place in the reading process.

In summary, what remains after removing the 'origins' of both myths and fairy tales is a need for a textual analysis that incorporates as necessary such factors as structure, content and context. Next, it seems clear that the story must be considered for what it is: a narrative system of signs based on convention – a semiotic system.

It seems that there are certain 'primary signifiers' which are used whose meaning is a complicated patterning in the emotional life and thought of the child. The further point is that the structure of affect in the story and of the signifiers in it 'suits' the child's needs at a particular moment in her life. Thus, the child makes sense out of the story vis-à-vis her context, and at the same time the story makes sense to her in her context. The affect structure of the story is, in some way, the material externalisation of an ineffable affectivity in the child, and the organisation of the signifiers in this structure *can* be used by the reader to 'mediate' this affectivity.

These primary signifiers which we cannot know prior to a reading are very important in the process of reading. Reading depends upon primary thought processes whose twin poles, according to Jakobson, are the same as language's: metaphor and metonymy. It is the use of these two tropes which I hope to show are the fundamental processes of reading *and* the conspiracy of the text.

The use of metaphor in comprehension has been shown by both Empson (1965) and Lacan (1972) to be the basis upon which meaning is actively invested into the text. Metaphor is a linguistic device which occurs when one signifier stands in the place of another in a text and where they share a common attribute or set of attributes.

From the reader's point of view the exploration of associations constitutes the meaning that the metaphorical construction generates; from this perspective it is more apposite to call these associations 'chains of signification', after Lacan (1972), in that it is by 'going down' these associations that the 'possible' meaning – the multitude of relationships that the signifiers can enter into – is explored or 'fleshed out'.

Empson (1965) makes a similar point when discussing the 'exploratory attention' demanded by metaphorical construction in poetry when he says that one must offer simultaneous translations in the various different directions that the chains of signification can take in order to dissolve the ambiguity of the poem. Lacan (1972) has pointed out, also in relation to poetry, that metaphor occurs at the precise point where sense comes out of nonsense; where the reader, recognising the metaphorical nature of the signifier in the text, can then explore its meaning or signification.

This brings me on to the relationship between reading and writing. The chains of signification that one uses to construct readings are not idiosyncratic to the reader, but public associations that link signs; they are conventional within the culture (langue) in which one has to grow up. In a sense, then, we can say that the presence of primary signifiers within fairy tales has metaphorical associative effects that the writer has put there in the first place:

As Culler (1975) points out: 'Even if the author does not think of readers, he is himself a reader of his own work and will not be satisfied with it unless he can read it as producing effects' (p. 116). For the author of any text to feel that he has written a particular text, he must have read and experienced it as such. This necessarily involves producing effects for others, that is, in the language of the other. Obviously one of the ways in which effects are created is through metaphorical construction, and the greater the disparity of the images signified, the greater the 'creative spark' and the greater the room for exploration for both reader and author.

It is now possible to point to the vital link between reading and writing, namely, that both are based upon the structure of language which allows, in a more or less constraining way, possible readings. On this account reading can be termed a re-writing. Indeed, reader's versions are re-written from the original text; because both texts depend upon the structure of language, then reading and writing can be identified.

One must, however, distinguish between the reading(s) and the text. The first is the meaning made out of the latter. I have shown that one of the ways this can be done is for the writer to construct metaphors and for the reader to recognise them as such and to explore the chains of signification. However, there is also the problem of the other constraint, that of the frame of reference and its relationships to the relatively ordered meanings that the metaphorical construction allows. It is with this larger question, that of the structure of the text and how it allows readings, that a structuralist poetics is concerned; it tries to make intelligible the underlying system which makes the text effective. This attempt must include all the possible meanings or the range of meanings of the text. Barthes puts it this way:

What interests it will be the variation of meaning generated, and, as it were, capable of being generated by works; it will not interpret symbols but describe their polyvalency. In short, its object will not be the full meanings of the work but on the

contrary the empty meaning which supports them all. (in
Culler, 1975, p. 118)

This 'empty meaning' is important for what constitutes its emptiness is the fact that it generates a set of meanings but is not itself
open to hermeneusis. This means that the possibility of a uni-
thematic reading, for example a moralistic or a sociological reading, is based upon the much larger problematic of the structure of
the language that the writer must necessarily use.

The study of the underlying system that allows this to happen
creates a science which goes beyond the individual and his relationship to his product (i.e. the text), as if the definitive ('full') meaning
resided in this relationship. In addition, it opens up the possibility
that the text is part of a system whose elements are other texts.

The underlying and organising concept that best characterises
this idea of reading as writing is the notion of coherence.[8] It should
be possible to ask: what makes a reading coherent? But this is now
the same as asking: what makes the text coherent? This arises
because the notion of coherence refers to coherence *for* a reader
and, as pointed out, a writer is a reader.

The intuitive answer to these questions is that it is the form of
the reading or text which gives coherence. Within structuralist poetics this idea of reading as coherence has various labels and con-
notations:

(i)   *Recuperation:* the association is of reviving a failing patient;
one that was almost lost.

(ii)   *Naturalisation:* what seems strange in the text is made habitual
and hence 'natural'.

(iii) *Motivation:* the process of reading whereby items that seem
random and incoherent gain coherence when seen in terms of their
functions and roles in the story as a whole.

(iv)   *Vraisemblablisation:* reading by using cultural models as

---

[8] The phrases 'relatively ordered' and 'more or less constrained'
refer to the fact that authors can direct very precisely a reader's
path down a particular chain of signification or can abstain from
so directing at all; compare for example Donne's 'A Valediction
Forbidding Mourning' in which his and his lover's 'soule'; 'If they
be two, they are two so/A striffe twin compasses are two/Thy soule
the fix foot, makes no show/To move, but, doth if the 'other do'
(here the reader is directed to certain attributes of the compass and
not others) with Shakespeare's notion of what happens on the Day
of Judgment: 'we ourselves compelled/Even to the teeth and fore-
head of our faults'. One can go a long way in many directions with
this (see Culler, 1975, pp. 182–3).

sources with which coherence is made out of the story.

All these words refer to 'ways of reading'. Their common denominator is that reading is an activity in which the reader makes use of frameworks with which to neutralise or *simplify* the text.

However, here again (and ironically when talking about reading as opposed to the 'higher ordered stimuli'), we come face to face with the obsession with the removal of the reader in his or her particularity.

What the structuralist poetic argument misses about reading is that each particular reader is going to produce a particular reading. This is certainly true when we consider children reading fairy tales. The discussion on Bettelheim shows that the 'framework' that will be used is affective. However, it is also true to say, along with the structuralists, that the use of this framework depends as much upon the 'underlying system' of the text as it does upon the context of the reader.

Furthermore, I will show in Part II that the affective framework is underpinned by primary signifiers which we can consider to be nodal in that they are vital positions in the chains of signification whose understanding by the researcher reveals where the reader is at a particular moment.

The meaning of these nodes is of course the links to other nodes in the system which create the desire on the part of the reader to 'find out about them' – that is to remove their ineffability which has the overall effect of a reduction in the potential plurality of meaning of the text because it is being used for a purpose in time.

1.6   The reader, the researcher and the text(s)

This Part I has been a necessarily skeletal presentation of both text and reading. The next section starts to fill out the model. Originally, in the thesis upon which this book is based, ideas developed as the data presented problems. This 'investigative method', that resolves contradictions as they arise, is often the actual way the research develops, and I will argue it is also the way reading 'works'.

Thus Part II is based upon this general approach. Figure 1.5 depicts the 'situation' of the research as it develops through this approach.

From Figure 1.5 it can be seen that vectors c, e, and d complicate the situation of the reader reading her favourite tale. This is because a set of conditions that have a meaning for the researcher are introduced, i.e. Y. It would be a delusion to pretend that the interaction of X and Y was not significant – few informants would

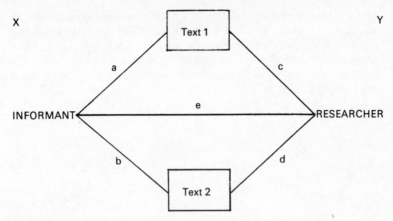

*Figure 1.5   The situation of the research where Text 1 is the
original story; Text 2 is the reconstruction*

be totally accepting of the interjection of a stranger into their world
and literature.

Vector c, d is based upon the text grammar. This means that
Text 2 is not a 'recall' in the sense that the informant is being
measured for memory capacity in terms of speed or accuracy;
rather, Text 2 is treated as another story which is a version of
the first text, in the same way that a myth has versions. Both c
and d presuppose the existence of a theory and practice of story
analysis.

Vector e is the channel of communication that carries the burden of messages designed to 'elicit' Text 2. It is also, in a very
intangible sense, the pathway through which the child feels reassured enough to want to talk to you. This *sounds* very messy but,
when it is admitted that the traditional subject of psychological
experiments *is* a subject, then one is imprisoned by 'inter-subjectivity'. However, it is only by operating within this prison that fruitful
research will be carried out. If there is no admission the closure of
inter-subjectivity and one's theory and methods are based in 'origins', the freedom gained will be illusory.

When this is taken into consideration, Figure 1.5 generates another methodological prerequisite, namely that Text 2 is embedded
in X along with the informant and Text 1. However, now the value
of inter-subjectivity becomes apparent simply because the researcher is also embedded in X and, using e, can now access those
conditions within which the child lives and which have meaning for
her. In order to find out about this larger 'text' (the context), it can
be seen that the use of vector e is extremely important. It cannot

be used for the passage of a rigid schedule of questions; rather the schedule is derived *in situ* from listening to the informant. All this is, of course, complicated even more by 'Y' which also demands a great deal of flexibility on the part of the researcher.

In what follows, an 8-year-old girl selects as her favourite fairy tale *Beauty and the Beast*.

Part II

Beauty and the Beast and its Reading

Appendix A shows how the levels of the model are related. In this section I want to take each SU in turn and describe them all in their vertical and horizontal dimensions as they function within the story.

2.1 The lure

The text is broadly divisible into two sections: the lure and the lesson. The first section is the lure and it lasts until SU 16 when the Beast's intentions become clear.

SUI
> Once upon a time there lived a rich merchant in a beautiful
> house with lovely gardens. He had four sons and three
> daughters of whom the two eldest, Marina and Rosina, were
> vain and lazy. They liked satin dresses and jewels. The
> youngest was Beauty, who was her father's pet. She was
> industrious, kind and loving to all.

Level of affect-signified: because this is the level where the decomposition starts all the SUs will be analysed from this point. Here, the affects are in opposition: selfishness v. selflessness. On the other hand there is in this SU a strong security which underwrites the opposed affects. This security is both affective and material.

Level of results: according to Benveniste (1971) the form of a unit is its composition in terms of lower units. The level of affect-signified's form is then composed, in part, by the next level below it, the results section. But here, at the very beginning, we run into a problem. It seems clear that we are working within a much larger unit, the introduction. The model is now faced with situating the grammatical units in the 'integrative' structure. Using Benveniste's notion of the form and the meaning of linguistic units, this particular GU, the introduction, has as its form opposed affects, and an *external inter-textual* result. But what is its meaning? In other words, what does it integrate? I would like to argue that, as grammatical, it has an overall integrative function in terms of the highest level of the text, the semiosis level. For Benveniste the notion of integration stops at the level of the sentence and starts at the level of distinctive features. This formulation of the grammatical unit (and indeed the whole model of the text) extends the twin notions of form and meaning as they were originally used by Benveniste as regards the sentence. I hope to show in the text that the GUs take on an important integrative function and I will, therefore, place it between the level of affect-signified and the level of semiosis.

Level of grammatical unit: I have stated above that this introduction has as part of its form an inter-textual result. But its coherence is also found in the culture generally because it is also the result of the reader's existential condition, mainly the desire to read a particular fairy tale or perhaps a result of the command: 'Go to your room and read!' By their very nature introductions are also transitions which have to get the reader out of her situation, school or home for example, into another one. This transitional nature of the introduction is the result of a certain fundamental 'way of doing' in society; we read and children read fairy tales. We have, therefore, another 'result' which I have termed cultural.

Level of propositions: the dramatic structure is descriptive.

Level of signifiers: these integrate the propositions. The case value of these signifiers in SU1 contains a lot of attributes, i.e. descriptions of characters, places and possessions.

Level of semiosis: the message proposed at this level is: 'This is a fairy tale.' The form of this level is all the other levels that lie beneath it. By looking closely at it we can see how it operates. It has the ability to use any level it wants to; it can 'dip' into them. So the primariness of 'once upon a time' and its case value is readily understandable in terms of the fairy tale code which is 'stable' in our language.

This, however, is not the only level that the S-level uses. The results level is needed because it is taken for granted by the text that this is not the first fairy tale the child has read (how children start to read these stories is another project). It is, therefore, an inter-textual result, a textual introduction which is part of a system of such introductions; 'once' and 'once upon a time' have been *read before*. So the coherence of the introduction is to be found externally in the inter-textual experience of the reader. The level of affect-signified is also used by the S-level in that fairy tales, according to the code, *are* about affective themes.

But the importance of the introduction should not be overlooked. It allows the reader 'to read' through the use of established codes. The 'meaning', in Benveniste's terminology, of this introduction is that it integrates the connotative message, *this is a fairy tale*: message, because it depends upon a code; connotative, because it 'uses' other levels of signification which are, in fact, other sign functions, (for example: affect-signifieds, 'once upon a time'). In fact we can see how the total SU1 is a connotor for this S-level message. Furthermore it is also possible to see how the form of this level is the other levels 'below' it. The signifiers integrate the dramatic structure of the propositions. These integrate the results which in turn integrate the affects signified which go up to make the introduction; all these levels contribute to the message: 'This is a fairy tale.'

In addition, the complications of SU1 have a functional role vis-à-vis the lure; SU1 must 'grab' the reader and take her from her existential situation into *another place*; in order to do this it relies on, in the first place, an extremely well-constructed and 'integrated' verticality and a very stable code.

SU2
The merchant lost his palace in a fire and his ships in a storm.
The family moved into a small cottage. The two vain daughters
grumbled about cooking and cleaning and coarse clothes.

This unit is less complicated vertically but now it is necessary to deal with the concatenation of SUs.

Level of affect-signified: there are two affects one of which is in direct opposition to this level in SU1 and the other is an insecurity coming from material lack that was part of the previous unit. Insecurity, caused by material lack, is opposed to the security that the merchant provided in the first unit. Selfishness, manifested in the daughters' grumbling, is carried over into this unit.

Generally, the affects of this unit are more straightforward and specific than in the first unit and for this reason it is part of a new grammatical unit.

Level of grammatical unit: this unit is called an *event* because of the specificity of the affect that is signified. An event is not an episode in that it is 'all of a piece'; there is no internal structure and, as a consequence, there is very little movement. Events state facts and generally give information.

Level of results: the event in SU2 is integrated by the specific affects mentioned above; part of the form of the event and the

affects levels is the set of results which integrate them. This set
consists of two external and one internal. The first external result
deals with the coherence of the destruction of the material well-
being and the second external result deals with the consequences
of this destruction. The first external result points to coherence in
the inter-textual experience of the reader; fairy tales are never
smooth running throughout. The second external result is an example of a 'cultural' result; when you are in a position of material
lack you cut down to size. In the present case you take smaller
accommodation.

The internal result allows the reader to understand the daughters'
grumbling; we know from the introduction that they are capable
of this type of behaviour.

Level of propositions: the overall impression is that information
is being stated, a factual structure.

Level of signifiers: this level integrates these propositions and
there is very little agency; it is also important that Beauty does *not*
appear here given the affects.[1]

Level of semiosis: once again the primary message here is to do
with the fairy tale code: 'Sometimes in fairy tales terrible events
happen.' It can be seen that once again at this highest level of
signification the text is relying upon a stable code to put its message
across. The reason for this is that the reader has been asked to do
a lot of work in making the story intelligible. So far there has been
only one internal and hence easily coherent result. The reader must
work hard at the beginning and the tale uses stable codes to 'keep'
the reader reading.

This is, of course, part of its narrative necessity in the service
of the lure. The text can also, in its concatenation of SUs, cross-
reference different levels; so the selfishness of the daughters mentioned in SU1 at the affect-signified level provides the internal
coherence at the level of results in this SU. This is termed an internal
result in the similarity mode; and I think it is not an accident from
the point of view of the 'lure' that the text uses once again
an extremely stable code and an internal result to 'hook' the reader.

SU3
 One year later the merchant heard that one ship is safe. He
 prepared to travel to the ship to get the gold yielded by the
 cargo.

---

[1] The textual and linguistic importance of the absence of certain
signifiers is discussed below when the function of 'absence' becomes
extremely significant. (See SUs 22 and 26.)

The reader has even more support immediately following as the story starts to balance its impact and at the same time progress.
Level of affect-signified: the balance is achieved on this level. What is proposed here by way of affect-signified is the 'hope' of security.
Level of the grammatical unit: this is the first part of a transition. As was mentioned in Section 1.4.7, transitions (including introductions) act to set the scene for the movement of characters and action within the story.
Level of results: there are two external and one internal. The first external result is the inter-textual one centred around the fact that other fairy tales propose possible solutions to problems. It is also 'logical' for the father to go and get the money from his ship.

The internal result is the coherence that centres around the 'security' affect; the hope of security here refers the reader back to the security of the introduction. It is, therefore, an internal coherence in the similarity mode.
Level of propositions: a dramatic scene of anticipation.
Level of signifiers: the dramatic structure of these signifiers is static but the verb 'prepared' gives the impression of impending movement.
Level of semiosis: once again the semiosis level can be seen to be in the service of the 'lure'. 'But fairy tales always leave a glimmer of hope.' If there were no hope (no transition out of the problem set by the introduction and the first event) then there would be no reading. At this highest level of reading the story is continually satisfying itself as a particular genre in which certain things will always happen.

SU4

The father asks the daughters what they want. Miranda wants dresses. Rosina wants jewels. Beauty wants her father's safety and a rose. He sets out.

Level of affect-signified: affectively this SU is a repetition of the introduction. We have here stated quite clearly the selfishness v. selflessness themes along with the promise of material security. Beauty's request makes the security complete.
Level of grammatical unit: this is the second part of the transition; the Father is now about to move. These transitions are in two parts because of the affect-signified which integrates them.
Level of results: there is a set of results which are wholly in the internal similarity mode; it is in fact the voice of the introduction.
Level of semiosis: significantly, this is the first time that the S-level has been allowed to communicate a message outside the

discourse of the text as either a general type or this particular example of the type.

This is an important point for both the text and its reading. The message at the S-level is built upon the affect-signified of security and selfishness. The message is: 'The father loves his daughter very much.' The code that condones this message is the stable father/daughter code which has as one of its rules the expression of affection for each other whether symbolically (the rose) or physically (kisses, for example).

On the other hand, it must be pointed out that the Father's actions are totally coherent within the story as well; the reader knows what a good father he is and especially of his affection for his 'pet' Beauty. What has happened here is that what is internally coherent has been made over into something which is socially intelligible; *all* fathers are like this.

Level of propositions: the dramatic structure is both anticipatory (we are still in the transitional unit) and descriptive.

Level of signifiers: the dramatic structure is interesting in that this is the first time the roles of the daughters have been clarified by the daughters themselves; we know their desires. So although there is the same affect-signified base as the introduction, the main difference here can be seen in the dramatic set-up of the signifiers, the manifestation of the affective themes.

Level of semiosis: here once again the text refers to itself not this time as genre but to a part of itself: 'Life could return to the introduction.'

The S-level relies on the results level but it is not so clear-cut as this. For example, it can be seen that what is coherent internally is the action of the girls and their desires which are intimately related to the affect level; i.e. we understand their requests because of the stated affective themes back in SU1. So, as mentioned above, coherence is internal in the similarity mode. The S-level gets its voice, as it were, from the results level and this level's relationship with the affect level. The S-level is speaking within the discourse of the text entirely and it is interesting to relate its message here to the message of SU3 where the 'glimmer of hope' message is now put into perspective by the text, i.e. a return to former times of full or complete security.

SU5

He discovers that the captain has stolen the money. He is disappointed for the children.

Level of affect-signified: this perspective is brought home to the reader at this level because of the familiar themes, insecurity and selfishness, and we can see that, affectively, the first two SUs are being repeated.

Level of grammatical unit: this is an event in much the same way SU2 was an event.

Level of results: the integration of the first two levels is carried out on this level by an external result of the cultural type ('people steal') and an internal similarity result in that the Father's disappointment is coherent from the affective theme of insecurity found in SU2.

Level of propositions: factual.

Level of signifiers: once again as with the other 'event' the dramatic structure is static.

Level of semiosis: the message here is similar to that of SU2, that things are not always smooth running in fairy tales. Here the message is simply 'remember the event' of SU2 and again the text does a double referring act. It refers to itself as a genre specimen and for this it relies on the fairy tale code and its stability. But it also refers to itself internally as the actual tale that is being read.

SU6

On his return he sees a castle of gold in lovely gardens. He sees a rose arbour and remembers his promise to Beauty. He picks a rose.

Level of affect-signified: Selflessness is the affect in that he goes out of his way to keep his promise to Beauty. This is the type of security that I term 'primary'; the desire for affirmation and recognition which this father's action is signifying, which is also underpinned in the beginning by material security.

Level of grammatical unit: this is the first part of an episode; it is not an event because of the fact that it will be internally structured. We can now get some idea of the reasons behind the double referring or reinforcing of the message that the reader is reading a fairy tale; the story is about to begin again and, until now, one general aim of the 'lure' has been to assure the reader that this really is a 'fairy tale'.

Level of results: there are two internal results both in the completion mode. The father returns because he went away and the picking of the rose is both a completion result and a similarity result in that the keeping of his promise completes it and at the same time we know this father is capable of keeping promises. The external result is inter-textual in that episodes happen in fairy tales.

Level of proposition: for the first time and, understandably given the grammatical unit, an 'action' dramatic structure.

Level of signifiers: the dramatic structure also reveals the action nature of the SU and it is obviously important that the Father picks the rose remembering Beauty.

The important point about SU6 is what it reveals about the operation of the text upon the reader; it brings what happens in the text to her life. Put another way, it transforms what is internally coherent (Beauty's father's action) into a social meaning.

As I mentioned in Part I there are two types of signification within the text:

(1)   The first is the signification found at the affect-signified level; we have the spectacle of the Father's gesture of affection for Beauty – he keeps his promise and picks a rose. He has been a model father in the past of the story; i.e. he is being internally consistent and the internal results level points to a similarity coherence at the affect-signified levels of previous SUs – especially the full security he provided before the loss of his house and ships. Type I significations are bound to the text.
(2)   Significations which rely upon a system of signification. These I shall call type II significations.

The third term as always is the reader's experience and, in some way, significations within the story must be made relevant to the reader and her experience *as they are read.*

SU6 provides a very clear example of this process at work. It is the first simple example of a process that will become more complicated as the lesson takes over the lure. The father's action – picking the rose while remembering Beauty – is intelligible in two ways:

(1)   Internally we know that he is capable of these actions; this coherence is given by the similarity mode of the internal result level; a type I signification.
(2)   Externally, in our culture's system of signification we know as readers that this is proper behaviour for fathers generally; the code here is the father/daughter and this is a type II signification.

How does the story get from I to II? The story relies on the two processes upon which language *itself* is based: metaphor and metonymy (both contiguity and synecdoche). This seems quite a 'natural' conclusion, given the reader is faced with a semiotic system. What happens is that the text allows the reader to make a simple substitution: Beauty's father for her father. Metaphor is a word for another word or what Jakobson (1978) calls selection: 'A selection between alternatives implies the possibility of substituting the one for the other, equivalent to the former in one respect and different from it in another' (p. 74).

The equivalence is that they are both fathers; the difference is that Beauty's father is not identical to the reader's father. Once the substitution has been made the reader can start to use the code of which fathers are a part. Jakobson points out that each selection is also part of a context, that is, it is in a relationship of contiguity to other signs. This contiguity can be of two types: either a contiguity of time and space in the spoken or written utterance or a continguity of part to whole (synecdoche). The first I shall call metonymy I and the second metonymy II. Metonymy is the motive force that allows the fleshing out, i.e. reconstructing the code of which father is a part (the father/daughter code in this example).

In a sense, of course, it is not the text that is holding out the possibility of substitution but language (the code) itself and what links reader and story is the commonality of the language. Most of the messages in the story found at the S-level have been made possible by very stable systems of signification. By far the most important has been the fairy tale code.

Even though the process of transforming type I into type II significations does not apply here the two modes of language do. Take for example SU1: we can see that 'once upon a time' is a fixed syntagm communicating that this is a fairy tale; on the other hand for the code to be reconstructed it must be realised that 'once upon a time' is only a selection of other beginnings, 'long, long ago', for example, that is, a process of metaphor but these selections from the code imply a context, the conventions that hold in fairy tale genre, i.e. 'once upon a time' stands for the *whole* genre (M II). This is a type II signification which has not been transformed; it relies on the external result whose modes point to where the code lies; here it is in the reader's inter-textual experience.

The important point about the role of metaphor and metonymy in thinking about the code is that, contrary to Saussure, Jakobson believes that these connections that the reader has the chance to make are already there concurrently in the language; for Jakobson (1978), Saussure 'succumbed to the traditional belief in the linear character of language "qui exclut la possibilité de prononcer deux elements à la fois",' (p. 75). The connections are there, yet it is up to the reader to make them. On the other hand the 'experienced' story knows full well that in its context Beauty's father has a very good chance of receiving the reader's father as substitute.

Furthermore, it goes without saying that these twin processes of language are also the twin processes of thought and Jakobson (and Halle, 1971) has remarked on their similarity to Freud's (1900) description of the primary processes of the unconscious, condensation and displacement.

How a particular reader fleshes out signifiers presented in the text, how she makes them relevant to her, depends upon these twin processes of language/thought – what they actually are depends upon the signifiers associated or labelled, and it is the role of codes to direct the exploration of signifiers in a socially acceptable way.

Consequently in SU6 the reader's interpretation of the message about the father in the story will be directed by the stable code of fathers and daughters. The connections will be possible because of the processes of metaphor and metonymy; the actual connection made will be due to the code.

The point is that the connections the text is going to make possible and those that the individual reader will make will be more or less coincident. In SU1 the coincidence of textual meaning and personal meaning is, in parts, quite close; this is because both are made possible by the *same* system of signification, the fairy tale code, as it is reconstructed using metaphor and metonymy.

But what about the other signifiers in the SU? If one takes, for example, 'kind', 'loving', or the 'father', they are also part of the fairy tale code; fairy tales are about affect and parents and children. But it is also clear that if the metaphor/metonymy is made with, say, father then there are further implications *for the reader* than simply the intertextual experience. 'Father' is part of a very complicated whole and the meaning of 'father' can now be seen as the links that are made to it. Meaning here, for a reader, is the *implications* of having started 'fleshing out' the whole of which 'father' is a significant part. From the point of view of the text connections are laid on and the *reading* depends upon and is structured by the reader's desire; the reader has to 'work' on the implications. This will only happen if there *is* a need/desire, an ineffable that needs articulating, in the reader; this is why she is reading the story.

I hope to show below that the text tries to mediate the reader's desire by insinuating certain systems of signification which articulate her experience for her; it makes the 'work' easier through offering her a structure.

One final point that comes out of SU6 is that of the constraints that are placed upon interpretation, the question of limiting semiosis. It can be seen that, as far as the text is concerned, the connotative message, because of the other levels (i.e. the form of the semiosis level), is exhaustive. The S-level is constrained by the particular nature of its verticality. But it is also constrained by the previous SUs, for example, those that describe the merchant (via the results section).

The other constraint is the existence of codes or sub-codes that direct the reader to certain connections and not others.

The final constraint is the experience of the reader and the use she will make of the invitation that the text holds out to her. This

last point of constraint should, of course, be in the secti
cerning the text's reception; its inclusion here indicates once
how difficult it is to talk of the text outside its reception or poss.
reception because the text is, after all, a semiotic system; furthermore, the text is *always* being read by me and the nature of its
structure is that it is *readable*. This is clear from the primary interface that the results section shows itself to be. Both types of results
function by pointing the reader in the right direction for finding
the coherence of a particular proposition or set of propositions.

External results point to an area of the reader's experience where
she could find the basis for rendering a proposition intelligible.
Internal results point to the past of the story and, of course, the
reader's memory of this past. But internal results also function by
telling the reader how to think about the proposition being read
through its various modes. Once this internal coherence has been
established the story transforms it into an 'external' codified signification through the use of metaphor and metonymy.

In the case of the present SU it can be seen that the metaphorical
switch of fathers, presented by the text, leads the reader to understanding what was originally internal to the story, the father's
action, in her own experience having to do with her father. The
story's father becomes intelligible because of the father/daughter
code reconstructed (possibly) in the metaphorical replacement. However, metonymically, the father is only part of a whole which may
be ineffable for the reader. As the story progresses it will be seen
that this whole will be filled out for the reader; whether she takes
it or not depends upon the peculiarity of her thought and problems.

SU7

A horrible Beast roars behind him. He has a head like a fierce
animal and the body of a man. The merchant is afraid and
tells his story.

The level of affect-signified: we have here the opposition from the
affect-signified of the last SU, viz insecurity.

Level of grammatical unit: the second part of the episode which
has a simple binary structure, integrated as it is by the affects.

Level of results: there are two results here. The first is an internal
result in the completion mode. The rationale for this is the title of
the story, *Beauty and the Beast*. He had to appear sooner or later
and his arrival completes, in much the same way as the promise of
SU6 was completed, something that was started at the very beginning. The second result is an external logical result. We know that
beasts *are* dangerous in nature and it is, therefore, quite intelligible
to be afraid.

Level of propositions: action and description.

Level of signifiers: dramatically it is quite simple, yet once again vital; the Beast roars at the merchant; the Beast is described.

Level of semiosis: this is the first time that this level is going to communicate two messages. There is on one level the connotative message that 'the Father will be punished for picking someone else's rose'. This is based, of course, on a particularly stable and explicit code, that of law and order. But the message that arises after this is in the form of a question to the reader: 'What is going to happen next?' These two connotative messages are in a strange relationship; on the one hand the law and order code firmly establishes the first message but the reader 'knows' from the title that the father will not die here; Beauty and the Beast are destined to meet and the father is the *key* to this meeting. Given this, another message arises which I have said is in the form of a question and it is related to the first message in that it is like a progression of thought; the father can't die so what happens next? But what code sanctions this message which is a question? What in fact allows the question to be read?

The answer here is the 'problem-to-be-solved code' mentioned above. In my opinion the child is facing problems both existential and textual; problems, that is, that concern her circumstances and that particular part of her circumstances called the story. After all, actually reading the story is an attempt at solving a problem facing her. Looking again at SU7, it can be seen that the second message of the S-level is asking a question, the meaning of which is assured by the above-mentioned code; it gets its meaning as a problem to be solved!

SU8

The Beast tells the merchant he will forgive him on one
condition. One daughter will come to live with him.

Level of affect-signified: the two familiar themes are represented selfishness v. selflessness.

Level of grammatical unit: this is the first part of a transition in that it sets the scene for the movement of the Father out of his situation.

Level of results: there is one external inter-textual result. The whole question of dilemmas and conditional statements is a fairy tale fact as is the demand for a daughter. Internally the reader is referred to the affective themes of selfishness v. selflessness that constantly recur.

Level of propositions: this is a conditional factual structure.

Level of signifiers: there is a straightforward dramatic relationship. The Beast is setting the condition and the merchant is receiving the message. Also only *one* daughter is asked for.

Level of semiosis: there are two messages here. The first is the familiar aspect of the S-level's function in the 'lure'; the reader is reassured about the fact that this is a fairy tale. The connotative message that follows is once again in the form of a question. The text has answered the question in SU7 with another question: 'What does the Beast want with one of the merchant's daughters?'

We can see that the primary signifiers 'one' and 'daughter' are important to this message; I have given 'daughter' a case value of (O) because, intuitively, the daughter is the proposed object of the Beast's desire. (Whatever, from the reader's point of view, that is!)

SU9

The merchant promises to tell his family. He promises to
return and be the Beast's servant if they refuse.

Level of affect-signified: the general affect here is – *inter alia* – insecurity which has been generated by uncertainty. This is combined with a certain 'selfishness' on the part of the father.

Level of grammatical unit: this is the second part of the transition.

Level of results: the promissory nature of the propositions is coherent internally as repetition, i.e., the father has made promises before. The unit is also understandable internally as a completion result; it is the father's answer to the dilemma posed in SU8. Externally the reader is referred to the fact that 'logically' the daughters are in a binary choice situation; they can refuse to go.

The most interesting result for the model is that internal similarity which renders intelligible the father's intended self-sacrifice. This is understandable because it refers to the kindness, etc., of the father that we already have seen; he provides well and keeps promises. It is interesting here because it is a clear example of another level from another part of the text being used to make a current SU readable. But it is *only* coherence that this gives; it is not the predominant affect-signified of this SU which remains as insecurity.

The conclusion is that propositions can be understood as belonging to the sequence of events of the story, its syntagm, through the use of another level in a previous column (for example, in this case the 'security' of SU1) but that this other signified is not necessarily given a privileged position at its 'proper' level (i.e. the affect-signified) in the SU being read.

Level of propositions: the structure is anticipatory and factual.

Level of signifiers: the father is doing the promising and he is the proposed agent of selfishness.

Level of semiosis: there are three messages connoted here. The first is sanctioned by the father/daughter code that we have already seen operating in SU6. The father's self-sacrifice is an example or token of this code (see SU21 for a discussion of the implications of tokens of codes to the reading process). The second message is sanctioned by the problem-solving code and elevated onto this is the third and last message that the reader is faced with: 'the plot is thickening' – the fairy tale code.

The message of the father's protectiveness, etc., through self-sacrifice is an example of the reinforcement of the transformation of this particular father into a general father and, possibly, into the reader's father. This was established back in SU6 and the reader is asked to think about whether this is an example of the code.

SU10

The sisters declare if Beauty had not asked for such a
ridiculous present, none of these misfortunes would have
happened.

Level of affect-signified: the insecurity of uncertainty that permeates SU9 is replaced by a different type of insecurity that contains the affects of blame and ridicule; it is insecurity of non-affirmation. Paired with this, though, is the familiar affect theme of selfishness – the sisters are graceless, to say the least. This 'paring' of insecurity and selfishness is no accident on the part of the text; it happened as well in SU5 and, in the general affect progression, the reader has been faced with the close association of these two affects.

Level of grammatical unit: this is the first part of an episode which, as I have pointed out, gets its meaning from the next part, together with its verticality.

Level of results: the internal result here is of the similarity type. We know from past experience that the sisters are capable of such declarations. The external result here is of the logical type in that, given the sisters' premise, then it follows that logically there would have been no trouble.

Level of propositions: factual.

Level of signifiers: again this is a straightforward dramatic set-up which is fundamental to the reading. It is clearly important that the sisters blame Beauty for what has happened; father could not.

Level of semiosis: the primary signifiers here contribute to the message: 'Beauty is responsible for getting the father into trouble.' The code is quite stable and moral: you are responsible for the other if you put that other in jeopardy, what could be called the 'responsibility' code.

SU11
   At last Beauty says she will go and live with the Beast to save
   her father. The father and brothers protest.

Level of affect-signified: Beauty's response signifies once again
another familiar pairing of affects; selflessness and insecurity (see
SU6).
Level of grammatical unit: this is the second part of the episode.
It is differentiated by the switch to 'selflessness'.
Level of results: one result, that of similarity. Beauty's kindness
and selflessness have already been stated and seen (her desire for a
rose).
Level of propositions: anticipatory.
Level of signifiers: a point of interest arises in this SU. Is the
Beast an object or a receiver (and therefore human)? This, of
course, is *the* question and it is clear that the case analysis of the
dramatic structure contains it; hence the case value of (O/R).
Level of semiosis: being responsible for the misfortunes; what
follows is quite reasonable. But here the S-level communicates exactly why Beauty gives herself up: 'Beauty feels responsible about
what she has done.'
   The code that sanctions the message is part and parcel of the
'responsibility' code of the last SU; having done something to jeo-
pardise the safety of the other, you make amends because you
should feel responsibility for what you have done. This I would
argue is certainly a sub-code in our culture. One does not have to
look far for the justification of this; the Christian faith is based
upon a love-thy-neighbour credo where respect for others and their
property is a paramount consideration. One can also see this working in the most obvious of codes: law and order. A point that I
should make here is that it seems clear that from now on in the
story it is going to be necessary 'to search for the code'; only a very
few social codes are actually written down in scriptures or law
books. Establishing a code is a research process which increases as
the stability of the code decreases. Nevertheless, the assumption is
that they are there.
   One can see here an example of the transition from a type I
signification to a type II. Beauty's selfless action is signified at the
affect-signified level and absolutely coherent internally; she's just
like that. But now the S-level offers the oppportunity for all little
girls to be that way (selfless) because of a codified sense of responsibility that one *ought* to feel if you've caused such or similar
situations.
   The reader is presented, by the story through the language, with
a thought: 'If I were Beauty (metaphor) would I do the same and

what would the implications be (metonymy II)?' The whole that the reader is being invited to fill out is that of her relationship with her father but directed by the 'responsibility' code.

SU12

> They set off and arrive at the castle which is already prepared for them. Beauty is charmed and they eat well. She almost forgets the Beast.

Level of affect-signified: familiar again is the hope of security that the text offers when things are particularly bad. It is for this reason that we are still in the 'lure'; it is of course a false affect, but the 'experienced' text does not want to lose its reader now.

Level of grammatical unit: this is a transition because it gets the couple from home to the castle.

Level of results: the first result is internal and simply completes the intended action of the last SU. The next result is external and depends upon the inter-textual reading of the reader where characters in fairy tales can have fore-knowledge; the last result is the internal similarity result which allows the reader to render intelligible Beauty's mood in that the material security of the introduction recalls for the reader this last part of SU12.

Level of propositions: action and descriptive.

Level of signifiers: the structure is again straightforward; Beauty features more than the father and it is significant for the whole SU (especially the affect-signified) that the Beast is *not* included.

Level of semiosis: the S-level this time is once again in the service of the 'lure'. One recalls the transitional SUs 3 and 4 where security features. In any case, the S-level is saying something like: 'Things may not be so bad.' We can see it is based upon the fairy tale code and is reinforced by other past examples of it in this story.

SU13

> They hear a tramp, tramp in the passage. Beauty clings to her father. The beast growls good evening to the old man and Beauty. Beauty is frightened but replies politely.

Level of affect-signified: the insecurity here is based in fear and it becomes understandable why the affect of the last SU was based in security.

Level of grammatical unit: this is the first part of an episode.

Level of results: the first result refers the reader to the fact that the Beast has to appear; they have come after all to his castle. Beauty clings to her father which is internally coherent from the S-level in SU9 but also externally coherent because of SUs 6 and

9 – the father/daughter code.[2] The growling of 'good evening' is external and cultural and the use of 'old man' is externally coherent from a logical point of view – fathers are old from the perspective of a little girl. Beauty's fear has a ring about it of the father's fear in SU7 and her reply is an external cultural result.

Level of propositions: action.

Level of signifiers: the 'power structure' of this SU – the father as powerless – is made clear by the cases of the signifiers. The Beast is always the agent; the other two are always receiving. Furthermore, the switch from father/merchant to old man supports this.

Level of semiosis: the semiosis level is important here mainly because we can see from the level of signifiers that this is the first time that the three main protagonists are dramatically related.

The message here must be seen in its relationship to the last S-level message which held out some sort of relief from the terrible situation that Beauty was walking into. This message at SU 13 is: 'But they could be.' This is sanctioned by the fairy tale code and also by past SUs which have a similar structure.

We can see here something of the constraint which the text itself places upon connotation. One could flesh out the implications of the primary signifiers and perhaps come out with messages other than the fact that things are going to get worse. The 'tramp, tramp', for example, could connote death and destruction; the growling could connote tearing apart. Although there is nothing to stop the reader doing this, it seems clear that the story would prefer to point the reader to other associations. Within the context of the story this SU has a particular title and it is, as we have been told constantly, a fairy tale. Death by shredding is hardly likely, even though there is nothing stopping this association being entertained by the reader – I just did it myself. Taken within the story though, all that can be said now is that the situation is worsening.

SU14

The Beast asks the merchant: did Beauty come willingly? The merchant says, yes. The Beast tells him to go first thing in the morning and never to venture near the castle; the old man leaves, full of grief.

Level of affect-signified: and it does get worse. The insecurity here is much more significant than the fear that permeated the last

---

[2] Results that refer the reader to an internal coherence when that coherence has been made external (i.e., from type I into type II) are from then on 'double edged'.

SU. This is insecurity through loss, what we call separation anxiety after Bowlby (1969), a primary insecurity.

Level of grammatical unit: this is the second part of a three-part episode. I have distinguished it from the first part because of the quality of the insecurity that is signified; that is to say the difference in the affect that integrates this SU, as opposed to SU13, is a difference that makes a difference.

Level of results: we know internally that Beauty did agree to come and live with the Beast; at one level of reading this was the result of her selflessness, but at another level of reading it was also intelligible as the result of a moral code of responsibility. These two combine to produce Beauty at the Beast's castle. The first result then is internal and in the similarity mode; in the first instance because of the theme of selflessness so closely attached to Beauty *and* because of the code concerning reparations at the S-level of SU11. This is the first example then of a type II signification being used by the text to support the possibility of coherence of another SU. The merchant's reply simply states the fact; she did agree to go and this is, therefore, an internal factual result.

The proposition in which the Beast tells the merchant to leave the castle is an internal result reliant on the S-level at SU8 which deals with the Beast's desire for one of the daughters; the old man leaving is simply the completion of the command and his grief is intelligible from what we know about him as a father.

Level of propositions: action.

Level of signifiers: the Beast remains in charge and it is only the old man who is full of grief.

Level of semiosis: built connotatively upon the insecurity of the loss of the father is the message: 'Why does the Beast want Beauty to be there willingly and without her father?' The code once again is the 'problem-to-be-solved code' which sanctions this as a question. It can be seen simply as an extension of the question the story posed in SU8; there are simply more conditions attached: the text is not answering anything just yet.

It can be seen here why this part of the episode is distinguished from the first part; it provides more information for the reader about the real basis for insecurity, separation anxiety, and the subsequent lack of recognition from one's father. This is a much more specific affect component of insecurity than that of fear (although fear is certainly part of it) which is more diffuse.

SU15
> One day in the garden a voice tells Beauty to be kind to the
> poor Beast and she will be happy.

Level of affect-signified: this is a familiar affect and it signifies to us that the 'lure' is still in operation.

Level of grammatical unit: this is an event integrated by the specific hope of security.

Level of results: the most obvious is the external inter-textual result; voices often speak to characters in tales; at any rate supernatural communication is quite possible. The rest of the SU relies on an external cultural result in that it is a way of doing in our society that we are kind to poor people/animals and we also know internally that Beauty *is* kind and has been happy because of it.

Level of propositions: factual.

Level of signifiers: the dramatic structure is static; it simply has Beauty listening to the promise of a happy future.

Level of semiosis: there are two messages here. The first deals with the fairy tale code but the second asks: 'Is the meaning of "kind" in this context being selfless?' This is sanctioned by the problem-to-be-solved code which makes this a question to be answered.

The primary signifiers, through a contiguous association, contribute to the message. For example, kind-poor-Beast are related metonymically (I). It is clear that 'kind' has throughout the story a close association with the affect-signified, 'selflessness', and that the attribute 'poor' cannot refer to the Beast's financial state but rather refers to his 'sad' state about which, so far, the reader knows nothing at all. Furthermore, the story is setting up a metonymy of contiguity *inter SU* between the father and the Beast; it is no accident that the father's grief is mentioned just before the Beast's sadness. What links them, of course, is Beauty and particularly Beauty's kindness. We can see this reflected in the case value for Beast where, being in a 'poor' state, he is much more a receiver than an object. Nevertheless, it seems to me that this message must be in the form of a question to the reader; this is what the reader is faced with, i.e. a series of messages in the form of questions-to-be-answered and it seems possible now that the meaning of signs like 'kind' and 'selflessness' are going to get other contents.

In a sense the main rule of the problem-to-be-solved code states that you have a problem when a discrepancy exists between a present state and a *desired* state whose fulfilling has a certain utility for the person; solving the problem involves a making congruent of these two states. In many ways this statement of the code is a brief summary of what psychologists who work in the area of problem-solving know. The difference is that any *exhaustive analysis* of the problem by the child, as is required or looked for in cognitive psychology's problem solving, is impossible simply because of the affective nature of it within the context of the story and what the child is trying to understand.

Now within the context of the story the reader is reading to mediate some problem; there is an interest or desire. This desire structures the reading (where she will go in exploring her chains of signification). But from the point of view of SU15 questions have been posed and what I hope to show is that it proposes to answer them for her; in a sense they construct her desire.

An interesting question is that if it is useful for the child to make these states congruent, then what is the utility for the text? One can only answer the conspirators behind the conspiracy of the text—a sort of cultural presence that directs the reader's reading.

SU16

Beauty admires the gold, dresses and jewels. The Beast seems quite gentle. He says 'Good evening' and he talks nicely. She sings to him. She says she is happy at the castle but she misses her sisters, brothers, and dear father.

Level of affect-signified; here the two grand themes are presented to the reader: on the one hand the material security that we have seen intermittently all along, on the other hand the insecurity (sadness) that has resulted because of the separation from her father. These two are opposed here and the SU shows an affective contradiction.

Level of grammatical unit: these affects integrate an episode part I.

Level of results: the first result is an internal inversion in that this is the first time we have seen Beauty being materialistic. The Beast's gentleness is cohesive internally in that he has been labelled 'poor' in the last SU, i.e. he has had a similar tag before. The 'good evening' is part of his repartee and, of course, part of our culture's. The fact that he talks nicely is intelligible internally through inversion; he growled before. Beauty's singing to him is both a cultural and internal result; women sing and especially in the 'once upon a time past' of the story. Internally we can understand this as a relaxation by Beauty because of the Beast's 'good manners'. Culturally we know too that you can be happy in circumstances of luxury. Yet we can understand Beauty's missing her family both internally (she loves her family – even the sisters), and culturally the reader can find evidence of people missing the warmth of the family and, for girls, especially that of the father.

Level of proposition: the overall dramatic effect of the propositions is action, as one would expect at the beginning of an episode.

Level of signifiers: the 'action' is integrated by signifiers whose case value is self-explanatory.

Level of semiosis: there are two messages here; the first is that 'the Beast is not harmful.' It seems quite clear that the Beast is being portrayed as a 'civilised' individual and the primary signifiers 'quite gentle', 'nicely' and 'good evening' are used by the S-level to connote the Beast's lack of threat and danger. The sub-code here is the 'civil' code which is probably part of a more general 'courtesy' code. However, the second message is again the major question, and it follows on from the first message. 'But what does he want with her?' The point is if he is not going to tear her apart, then what is he going to do? This relies on the 'discrepancy' rule; there is still a vital lack of information which the reader, who continues to read, will want to know.

With this SU we come to the end of the 'lure'. The reason for this division here is, of course, because of its relationship to the next SU but also because SU 16 presents the major themes of affect and the vital S-level question. Beauty is in a situation in which she is only half made-up, materially secure but emotionally out of balance because of the loss of her father. My contention is that the story knows this too and will attempt to 'fill up' the other half in a way that suits it.

2.2   The lesson

SU17

The Beast asks Beauty to marry him and always live there as
the mistress of the beautiful palace. Beauty says 'no' in horror.
The Beast sighs and tells Beauty to have pleasant dreams.

Level of affect-signified: the shock-horror here is unmistakable but it is not clear at this level why she is horrified.

Level of grammatical unit: this is the second part of the episode that tries to complete the first part – the emotional lack – but it is integrated by an even more powerful insecurity.

Level of results: The Beast's proposal, from a naive point of view, comes as a surprise. This is only true, however, if you ignore the S-level because internally from SU15 the answer of 'kind' is being fleshed out. There is here then an answer (partial as we shall see) to the question of SU15. This is, therefore, a completion result. That he should go on and ask her to be mistress of the palace can be found intelligible externally in the culture, i.e. the housewife. However, that it should be a palace is hard to understand. One place to look for coherence is the inter-textual type of external result; people in fairy tales have been known to live in palaces. But it is also true that her house that burnt to the ground was described as a palace (SU2). In this case the reader is asked to search her

memory of the story for a palace and when she arrives she will see
that it is her father's palace that was destroyed. All that the text is
depending upon here is the reader's memory of the introduction
and first event and, as a consequence, the metaphorical association
is presented as possible. This is an internal similarity result in that
Beauty lived in a palace before as her father's pet – not quite the
mistress but certainly the favoured female for reasons the reader
knows a lot about.

Where does the coherence for Beauty's answer lie? In the first
place, although the Beast has been 'civilised' by the story, one has
to draw the line somewhere; after all, he *is* a Beast. However,
Beauty's answer is tagged with such a strong affect that the coherence for this cannot be entirely internal just because of the fact
that the story has been humanising the Beast.

The child reader is then faced with a problem. It is this: where
does she look in order to render intelligible the security of Beauty's
rejection of the Beast's offer of marriage? It must, in part, be
external and it must be in the cultural mode. It seems clear that
coherence centres around the word 'marriage' and its meaning. So
the reader must look around in her 'ways of doing' catalogue of
experience for what *she* means by marriage.

The Beast's sigh is external and cultural – the result of rejection
and his wish of pleasant dreams is likewise an external cultural
result – it is a way of saying good night, usually, to children.

Level of propositions: the overall dramatic effect is that of action.

Level of signifiers: the action is integrated by signifiers marked
by adverbs, attributes and verbs of action. It seems obvious but
worth stating that it is necessary for any significance at all in this
SU that the Beast does the asking and Beauty does the answering.

Level of semiosis: it is at this level, integrated as it is by the other
levels (which make up its form), that the loose ends of these other
levels can be tied up.

The first connotative message is: 'The meaning of being kind is
marrying the Beast.' Here, through an internal completion result,
we have a 'lateral' connotative message where the question posed
at the S-level of SU15 is being answered by the story. But what
does it replace 'kind' with? The answer is the word 'marry' and
this, in turn, sets up yet another (but from the point of view of the
text infinitely more important) connotative message in the form of
a question: 'But what is the meaning of "marry"?' The basis for
this is the search that the text sends the reader on within her
signifying structure. When she arrives at the word 'marriage' she
may or may not have firm connections with it. What we can say
for sure now is that the text is offering her, through a contiguous
metonymy in the mode of a question/answer style, the link:

kind = marry. On the other hand, the reader has the possibility of knowing that 'kind' is also related to the continual theme of selflessness (which of course gets its meaning from its opposition to selfishness). So the link that is now possible is: kind = selflessness = marry. It is important to note that the text has not made this equation very coherent, but this is just the point, it is about to and is going to be the substance of the 'lesson'.

This is why I think there is a 'natural' break in the narrative. SU16 has presented to the reader two opposing and seminal affective themes which are quite coherent given the past of the story. It is as if SU16 represents the introduction but this time with a lack or an emptiness. The story is going to try to fill this emptiness and SU17 is the beginning of a lesson in which the story will offer the reader a difficult, yet possible, way of balancing the affective imbalance found in SU16. Furthermore, it can be seen that, in SU17, the transfer of signification found within the story (type I) into a signification in the child's life (type II) is once more being set up. The reader is being asked to think about marriage and marrying with the help of 'being kind' and 'being selfless'; the story is given a meaning to a signifier and it will be remembered that in SU9 a similar process was taking place. However, in that SU the text relied upon a very stable code, the father/daughter, to effect its possible metaphorical and metonymical connections. SU17, on the other hand, presents the reader with an unintelligibility, the meaning of 'marry' (given Beauty's violent reaction); not having a stable code to produce the desired signification, the text is going to lead the reader to an understanding of this word.[3]

The way it starts to do this is to give the reader possible metaphors and metonymies; it starts thinking for her and, through the problem-solving code, invites her to participate. What it now has to do is solidify those connections until they are accepted or received, i.e. socially conventionalised.

SU18

For some months Beauty lives in the comfort of the castle.
Each evening the Beast asks Beauty to marry him. She always
says 'no'. The Beast becomes sadder and sadder until Beauty
feels quite sorry for him.

Level of affect signified: the shock horror of the last SU is followed by a restatement of the themes but this time one is formed

---

[3] The point is that the story knows that the code of which 'marry' is a main signifier is not clear, or well labelled, in any child who is attached to this text.

from a different affect. The material security is restated by the insecurity is formed by sadness; the sadness is the Beast's because of his rejection and the concommitant sorrow of Beauty.

Level of grammatical unit: these affects integrate the third part of this episode and in order to understand the relationships of these affects it is necessary to see them within the structure of the whole episode and indeed the story itself. The text starts to become very complicated.

Level of results: the first is an internal repetition in that her being there and him asking her to marry had happened before. The Beast's sadness is understandable externally in the culture in that this is one expression of rejection. Beauty's reaction is intelligible in two areas: the first is internal in that we know as readers that Beauty is 'kind to all' and has an astonishing capacity to give; the second is that culturally Beauty is making the proper reaction to someone's sadness.

Level of proposition: the overall dramatic effect is static (factual) and descriptive.

Level of signifiers: the descriptive nature of the propositions is integrated by signifiers which include a lot of adverbs, attributes and time cases.

Level of semiosis: at the first level of connotation there is a message which continues with the Beast's humanisation: 'The Beast has emotions just like a human.' The code that sanctions this message is the fairly stable rule that says that people express sadness when they are rejected; the unrequited lover rule, if you will. The second message that arises from this is: 'Beauty is the cause of the Beast's distress.' This arises from the first message and is sanctioned by the same code in that for a lover to be unrequited there must be an 'unrequiter' who is responsible for the 'unrequited's' misery.

This progressive humanisation of the Beast is quite understandable. His elevation to humanity is part of the process of making a type I to a type II signification being established here by the 'unrequited lovers code', and it seems clear that the story has as one of its goals the presentation of the Beast as potential marrying material. How the text will do this can only be seen when these first three parts of the episode are seen in relationship to the next SU which acts as both a completion to the episode and a transition.

SU19
During this time Beauty often thought of her father. One day she looked into a magic mirror. She saw her father lying ill in bed. She becomes sad.

Level of affect-signified: affectively this represents a return to the type of insecurity found in SU17; the loss of the father and the sadness at the separation.

Level of grammatical unit: this affect integrates a transition part (I) in that the story is preparing the reader (and Beauty) for a shift of scene.

Level of results: the first result is internal similarity because we know that Beauty misses her father. However, this result is double-edged because its coherence is also external and cultural – little girls in similar situations would think of their fathers quite a lot.

The story itself has sanctioned this latter type of search in SU6 where the transformation of type I to type II signification was completed within the stable father/daughter code. So, having been transformed once via a stable code, external searches from then on may be legitimised by the story (this is still only in the story's structure, and I am not making any statement about what the reader has made of the father before SU6; it is just that, at SU6 the possibility of associating the 'story' father with the reader's father becomes socially potential rather than simply a set of idio-syncratic associations).

Seeing her father in a magic mirror is external and inter-textual and internally a completion result; she thinks of her father and then she sees him. Rendering intelligible the father's illness can be found in the fact that, in the story, he has been tagged as an 'old man' and at the same time 'old men' are ill (die) in our culture (external: cultural). Beauty's sadness is also both internal because she is capable, with her father, of this emotion and external cultural because of the story's previous transformation of the text's father/daughter dyad into culture's father/daughter dyad.

Level of propositions: this SU is mainly factual in that it states something that happened concurrently.

Level of signifiers: Beauty is seen with most of the agency; her father is the receiver, and it is obviously important that the Beast does not figure in this SU.

Level of semiosis: the first message that is connoted is that: 'This is still a fairy tale.' This arises from the 'magic mirror'. I would argue that this is more a 'stylistic' device on the part of the text in order to effect the transition than a reminder to the reader that she is still reading a fairy tale; nevertheless the message is clearly there to be grasped.

The second message is something like: 'The father's illness brings out Beauty's kindness.' This is so because of its relationship at the S-level that preceded it; Beauty is being unkind to the Beast. What is the code? The code is still one that deals with the relationship of fathers to daughters in our society. However, instead of it being the way it was in SU9, it is now a rule about how daughters *should* behave towards fathers when they are in some sort of distress; we must be kind to (respect) our fathers. This message is, of course, integrated by various levels and SUs in the story; Beauty is kind and has been kind to her father; she is a preterpluperfect daughter.

However, the interesting thing here is to see these four SUs schematically to illustrate what the text has in mind vis-à-vis the father and the Beast and, of course, Beauty.

The following table shows the text once again delighting in the process of metaphor/metonymy.

Schematic representation of SUs 16/17/18/19.

SU	16		17	18	19
S-level	Why does he want Beauty alone with him?	+	Marrying = kind = selfless	Beauty is being unkind to Beast	v. Beauty is kind to Father
Affect-signified:	Sadness (Separation)	v.	Shock horror	Sadness Sorrow	+ Sadness Sorrow
Primary signifiers:	Dear Father	v.	Marry the Beast	Beast	+ Father

The relationship between 16 and 17 is best described as an attempt to fill up the emptiness created by the separation. So at the S-level, a question is answered, a type of filling up. At the affect-signified level the 'emptiness of separation' is filled with fear. At the level of primary signifiers there is an attempt at a replacement of father for the Beast; this fails miserably and we can place an opposition sign between them.

The relationship between 18 and 19 at the S-level is an opposition unkindness v. kindness. At the affect-signified level there is identical affect, and it is through this identification that at the primary signifier level Beast is metonymically linked to father. Where the relationship of 16 and 17 fails because of the shock horror, it succeeds in the relationship of 18 and 19 because of the sadness Beauty feels. The opposition remains at the S-level but starts to disappear at the level of the affect-signifieds and signifier. Beauty feels 'during this time' the same emotions for both the Beast and her father, but the contradiction is that she is being unkind to the Beast by rejecting him and kind to her father. A mediation is, therefore, called for by the text at the S-level.

SU20

　　Next day Beauty asks the Beast to let her go home, for a little while, to see her father again and her brothers and sisters. The

Beast is grieved as he loves Beauty so much. At last he agrees but Beauty must promise faithfully to return in two months or she may find him dead. He gives her a ring to return to the castle.

Level of affect-signified: the attempt at mediation begins here with a restatement of the dominant affective themes; the security of the father's presence opposed to the insecurity of the Beast's possible death; from the identification of affect in the last two SUs we now come to an opposition centred around the father and the Beast.

Level of grammatical unit: this is the second part of the transition in which Beauty actually sets off for home. It seems reasonable that the transition should be integrated by opposing affects (see 4 and 8) in that Beauty is leaving one place for another place and that these two places get their meaning from the affective difference.

Level of results: the first is internal and completing because she does want to see her father. Internally similar is the Beast's sadness and his eventual agreement is internally coherent in that he is not such a bad person. It is also coherent internally that he should set conditions; he has done it before and the content of his conditions can be understood internally because of his desire to marry Beauty. The giving of the ring is inter-textual and that she sets out is a completion of the whole transition.

Level of propositions: obviously this is a conditional SU.

Level of signifiers: obvious, but important, that the Beast sets the conditions to Beauty's request and that she has to promise him faithfully to keep her end of the bargain.

Level of semiosis: the first message must be to the effect that the Beast is really quite a nice person; we know that the story has been progressively elevating him to human-ness and he shows a certain kindness that is part and parcel of a fairly amorphous 'decency-civil' code that has been seen before in SU16. It follows from this that Beauty cannot let him die and that 'they will see each other again' is a possible message reinforced as it were by the extremely stable code about keeping promises/honesty, etc. The giving of the magic ring generates the third message that this is a fairy tale. There is a theme at all the levels of connotation in this SU that supports the Beast's survival – it would be a cruel trick if the conspirators behind the story killed the Beast off through Beauty's indifference – but of course that is not the intention as we shall see.

SU21

She arrives and the family is happy. Beauty runs to her father's room and, seeing her, he soon recovers. He asks if the Beast treated her kindly. After she tells her father all he wanted to know she shows Miranda and Rosina the beautiful presents she brought them and precious things for her brothers and a chest of gold for her father.

Level of affect-signified: at home there is a resolution of the two opposed affects into total security, material and that of recognition/ affirmation. But where these exist, selfishness and selflessness can't be far behind.

Level of grammatical unit: this is the first part of an episode.

Level of results: that she arrives is a completion; running to her father is double-edged both similar and culturally coherent. His recovery is coherent internally in that he loves her and this is culturally also coherent.

The asking of questions is a culturally coherent result in that fathers do ask about daughter's activities; the concern is also internal because the last time that there was father interaction with the Beast the latter growled at him. The giving of presents is a good restatement of Beauty's kindness (selflessness) and the introduction generally; that she should bring these things is an internal and factual result – the family *is* poor.

Level of propositions: the dramatic structure is active.

Level of signifiers: Beauty arrives and gives, runs to her father and he recovers; all extremely important dramatic relationships which provide the basis for any signification at all.

Level of semiosis: Two messages: 'The father was ill because he missed Beauty' and, built on the security, 'Everything is all right again.'

The stability of the father/daughter code – its labelling of the metaphors – ensures the first message, whereas the second is connoted largely through the memory of the introduction – for in fact this SU is but a variation on it.

SU22

Two happy months pass quickly. Beauty begins to think of her promise to the Beast. Her brothers beg her to stay on. She puts off going back to the castle.

Level of affect-signified: the main affect here is the selfishness Beauty generates from trying to keep the security of SU19.

Level of grammatical unit: the second part of the episode integrated by opposing affects.

Level of results: the first is a completion result; she made the promise and it is simply a completion of an earlier action. That her brothers want her to stay is internally coherent in the similarity mode – they did not want her to go in the first place. This is also intelligible externally in our culture in that family cohesion is part of our experience. She puts off going back because we know as readers that she is happy, and her action is also comprehensible internally as an inversion; it is contrary to expectation that Beauty should break a promise.

Level of propositions: dramatic structure is rather static and it states certain facts.

Level of signifiers: important here is the fact that only the brothers ask her to stay. This is extremely important in that we know for a fact that the story would lose all credence from the point of view of the affective themes of selflessness v. selfishness if the sisters asked her to stay. The brothers are key signifiers from the point of view of the coherence of the narrative.

Level of semiosis: the brothers are not, however, particularly primary for this level. The message here is a straight connotation from the affect-signified level: 'Beauty is being selfish by breaking her promise to the Beast.' This is an example from the 'keeping one's promise code' which is stable not only in the adult world, 'my word's as good as my bond' but more important in the child's world where breaking a promise is a terrible crime.

SU23

> One night Beauty has a terrible dream. The Beast is lying ill under a large tree. She hears a voice: 'You have broken your promise, Beauty, and see what has happened.' Beauty is frightened and uses the ring to go to the castle.

Level of affect-signified: the SU is filled with Beauty's guilt which is the result of her selfishness.

Level of grammatical unit: the first part of a transition which will move her (guilt is a powerful motive force).

Level of results: that we dream is a cultural part of our experience. It is also internal in that she has been wished pleasant dreams (17). The Beast lying ill under a tree is a completion result; he warned her he might die. She hears a voice; she's heard them before (similarity) and dreams include dialogue (cultural). The fact that the voice says, 'See what you have done', is an internal factual result in that it is a fact that if she broke the promise this would be the outcome is a completion result. Beauty's fear is a cultural reaction to causing someone's illness and the use of the ring is a completion result.

Level of propositions: dramatically this is very active.

Level of signifiers: the inclusion of the voice which does the speaking is significant because of its association with the voice that talked about being 'kind' to the Beast. So, where it all happens, under a tree, in a garden, one assumes, is important; and it is obviously important that Beauty has the dream and it is about the Beast and his predicament.

Level of semiosis: the message here is quite straightforward – 'Beauty feels responsible for the Beast's illness.' The code is the same that appeared in SU10; you are responsible for the other if you put the other in jeopardy. But unlike SU10 where Beauty was made to feel selfish by her sisters, here she does it all by herself – or rather the code does it for her; it *makes* her feel guilty.

With this SU the replacement by the story of the father by the Beast is clinched. They are inseparably linked by the code of 'responsibility to the other'; but in order to do this Beauty had to feel guilty – an extremely 'social' emotion.

SU24

She cannot find the Beast in the castle. At last in the evening Beauty runs into the garden weeping and calling his name. She comes to a tree, like the one in her dream. She sees the Beast lying, face down, apparently dead; she is horrified. She runs for some water to revive him.

Level of affect-signified: following the guilt comes the anxiety; the story is putting Beauty through a wringer.

Level of grammatical unit: the second part of this transition. Beauty arrives motivated as she is by her guilt.

Level of results: she cannot find the Beast in the castle because we know that he is in the garden (internal: logical); when driven by guilt and anxiety logic is not someone's strong point. Running into the garden is the completion result – he is after all under a tree; calling and weeping is internally coherent in that she is guilty and anxious. On the other hand Beauty is now an examplar of how to handle these emotions so the reader is also asked to search externally for 'ways of doing' (see the S-level).

Seeing the Beast lying on the ground is a completion result and being horrified is intelligible internally and culturally; this time, however, Beauty's horror, something she seems to be capable of (see SU17), is at what she has done to the Beast, not as in 17, what he did or proposed to do to her, i.e. marry him. So we have a similar emotion felt by the same person but in inverse circumstances (dramatic structure has been inverted). The last result is an external logical result; water does revive people.

Level of propositions: the dramatic structure is active.

Level of signifiers: the adverbs of weeping and calling are vital; Beauty's agency in all this is also important.

Level of semiosis: the message here is: 'Beauty is suffering for what she has done to the Beast.' The code? Once again this is part of the code complex, an *example* of what happens after you have jeopardised the other – you act in this way, i.e. weeping, crying; in a word you *suffer*. This is in a way a 'natural' behaviour – it is a codified way of doing in our society.

SU25
At last he opens his eyes. He is delighted to see Beauty again.
He tells her he will have supper with her that night.

Level of affect-signified: relief – the Beast is not dead after all. This emotion makes Beauty feel secure again – she did not after all kill the Beast.

Level of grammatical unit: the first part of an episode.

Level of results: the opening of the eyes is a completion result from the giving of the water to revive him. His delight is, of course, internal and similar and having supper is a repetition.

Level of propositions: an active dramatic set-up.

Level of signifiers: quite straightforward from the case point of view.

Level of semiosis: the first message here is: 'Beauty makes amends by saving the Beast's life.' This is sanctioned by the responsibility moral code which require that, having done harm to another, you 'pay back' in some way. Our culture can be seen as very generally being one where reciprocation is the *leit motif*. Criminals pay debts to society; the villain, if he does not make amends, will have a terrible fate; 'crime does not pay'; this is so in a lot of fairy tales as well. One only has to recall the fate of the Wicked Witch of the West in the Wizard of Oz when she tricked Dorothy out of her shoes for her greedy desire. It is also an important part of growing up in that one is taught to respect the other and his property.

Not respecting him or her leads to reparations but the feeling of *guilt* is what is instilled to make these reparations possible; that is what I meant when I said above that guilt was a particularly social emotion and so, of course, is the concommitant anxiety.

The second message is sanctioned by the problem solving code: 'Why is he having supper with her?' The answer seems obvious and I think it is intended to be so. Nevertheless, the reader is still faced with the question.

SU26
After supper the Beast asks Beauty to marry him. She answers 'Yes, dear Beast, I love you very much.' The Beast is surprised.

Level of affect-signified: instead of the horror we saw in SU17 in the same circumstances we now have love – the ultimate form of security.

Level of grammatical unit: the second part of the episode; the relief from the burden of guilt is followed by love and recognition.

Level of results: the asking to marry is a simple internal repetitive result. Now, however, comes the crunch as far as the whole story and in particular the results section is concerned. How does the reader render intelligible Beauty's affirmative reply and her declaration of love?

Internally we have seen how the Beast was not only humanised but he became a substitute for the father; the Beast is a metaphor for the father. It is, therefore, very easy, if this is so (i.e. the story's been successful in effecting the substitution), to switch one's emotions onto the replacement, i.e. be kind/selfless to the Beast; we have already seen how this is possible in SUs 18 and 19. But this, one might argue, cannot be enough and that would be right; Beauty's declaration of love is not simply because father was cunningly associated with the Beast and vice versa but because she also *felt guilty.* The coherence for this is found in the story from SU10 onwards where responsibility and selflessness are related in an episode dealing with Beauty getting her father into trouble and where one's moral responsibility toward the *security* of the other was the message.[4] On the other hand you could not, as a little girl, give yourself to an animal, a Beast; but you could if he was as cleverly associated with father as this Beast has been.

Level of propositions: an active dramatic scene.

Level of signifiers: simple, straightforward asking and receiving.

Level of semiosis: the message is: 'Saving the Beast's life is not enough, Beauty must also marry and love him.' In order to establish the code that sanctions this message it is necessary to take a general look at the story until now.

One of the major accomplishments so far has been the substitution (metaphor) of the Beast for the father; the story has managed this through metonymies of contiguity. For example SUs 18 and 19 quite clearly showed that Beauty's sadness was simultaneously associated with the Beast and the father. Recently we have seen the spectacle of Beauty saving both the father and Beast. All this has

---

[4] From the point of view of security/insecurity they are related to guilt, and anxiety (*inter alia*) as primary is related to secondary; the former are basic the latter contingent. It is difficult to imagine a society where people did not need recognition as people but not difficult to imagine a society where guilt was a socially necessary concommitant.

gone on with the Beast's habilitation into a human being since the 'old man' left the castle.

Having made the substitution possible, Beast for father, the story also makes another type of metonymy possible, that of a synecdoche, or part for whole. In other words by making the Beast a metaphor for the father, he has also become a part of the whole of which the father is a part.

The main attribute that links these two is that they are both *men*. In a sense, the Beast is like the father but not identical to the father. This is obviously an important point because the message of the S-level has to do with the love and affection of Beauty and upon whom she bestows it – someone whom the story has made into a being like her father but not exactly her father.

All this revolves around the primary signifier of 'marriage' and the signification it is given in the story. I would like to propose that the story is working to codify a set of signifiers some of which have affective signifieds. At the heart of these is 'guilt'. It seems clear that the moral/responsibility code which deals with responsibility for the other is being insinuated into an area of the language that has, as one of its main signifiers, 'marriage'. The story has been preparing the reader for the metonymies of marriage, i.e. kindness and selflessness. The Beast, as I mentioned above, has been set up as acceptable marriage material. All that remains is to get her to marry the Beast; the motive force is guilt. The code is saying: women (girls) when feeling guilty about their responsibility to men concerning questions of 'marriage' must make amends by capitulation – agreeing, that is, to their demands.

We can distill the associations to men – guilt – marriage. The story has not in any way emitted messages of an explicitly sexual nature; the important point is that it does not have to. The metonymies around 'marriage' for a little girl reader will fill this gap up. We have been formally aware, since Freud (1905), of children's speculation about sexuality; being married is what mother and father are; she is the mistress of the house (palace) and the state of being married is a whole series of metonymies centred around mother and father and their activities, especially those that occur without the children. Furthermore, it is no accident that absent from the text *but not from the language* is the mother; if the Beast is a man not unlike her father then marrying the Beast makes Beauty a woman not unlike her mother. The inclusion of the mother in the narrative would have made nonsense of the strength of Beauty's feelings for her father and the subsequent switching of them onto the Beast – another female who gives, is kind, selfless, etc., to the father would not have allowed the dramatic effect; *'mother' would have got in the way.*

It is an important notion that what is left out of a story is as important as the relationships actualised in the story. Linguistically on the other hand, according to Jakobson (1971), everything is present at once. The enunciation of father has simultaneous associations with mother (etc.) in the language.

The associations then to marriage, before reading *Beauty and the Beast*, could be re-structured after reading it. 'Marriage' starts to take on a meaning and most importantly for the reader her feelings of kindness, love and *guilt* also start to take on a meaning.

The most important feeling that the story is dealing with is the love and affection that the daughter feels for the father and, from the daughter's point of view, her father's feelings for her. The story established this back in SU6 as a type II signification; these mutual feelings are a well-established social practice. The story's achievement is to switch this affect (or rather to present the possibility of switching) onto someone who is like the father but who is not quite identical, yet at a price; Beauty is made to feel guilty. It is not only Beauty who feels this way. We have seen as readers why she acts like this; her behaviour is internally coherent (if not consistent). On the other hand this behaviour receives social sanction at the S-level, and we can see the ultimate purpose of this story; a type I signification has been exteriorised into a type II: this is the way all little girls should behave. It is very much the same process that we saw in the Wizard; what drives Beauty into loving and marrying the Beast is not so much her guilt about what she has done to him but the code that tells her what to do about it!

However, it is not enough to establish the code only in the story; what must be done is to establish the code for what it is, i.e. a socially conventionalised rule. One of the places to look for this code is in our literature about women. Diana Trilling (1978) presents what could be called a corollary to the rule mentioned above. She points out that within the body of our literature from the Greeks to the present time the concept of the liberated heroine – generally that female character in a novel or play who would try to act and create her own space, and fail – means women who:

> ... have subdued their personal needs to others ... heroine-ism
> ... is seldom demonstrated in action, or not in freely elected
> action. Heroines are in the first instance women who please,
> help and wait. They please men and are helpful to them in
> their undertakings. (p. 163)

One of the great heroines is Emma Bovary, who is punished severely for the *hubris* of wanting something different from the life that the insipid Charles could give her. I would point out that it was not so much Flaubert who killed Emma off but the social code; Emma's sin was not so much her extra-martial sexual activities but her not looking after Charles like a good wife, caring for him and feeling for him.

Although the reason for the marriage has very little of the code in it, the life she leads almost immediately after it confuses her original feelings for Charles:

> Before the wedding, she had believed herself in love. But not having obtained the happiness that should have resulted from that love, she now fancied that she must have been mistaken. And Emma wondered exactly what was meant in life by the words 'bliss', 'passion', 'ecstasy', which had looked so beautiful in books. (Flaubert, 1970, p. 47)

One is led to wonder what books she actually read as a little girl; it could very well be that these signifiers were related through guilt and selflessness in much the same way as *Beauty and the Beast*.

In any case the point is made that in literature marriages are often underpinned by the women's selflessness. Eliot's Dorothea Brooke marries Casaubon in order to help his literary career instead of making her own, as Eliot says:

> Dorothea's inferences may seem large; but really life could never have gone on at any period but for this liberal allowance of conclusions, which has facilitated marriages under the difficulties of civilisation. (in Trilling, p. 47)

It seems clear that the capitulation of women is manifest in the literature that is based, in part, on women trying not to capitulate; they fail; they are killed off and held up to ridicule. Better in fact to *give in*.

From my point of view they have little other choice. Emma Bovary did not burst fully grown onto the pages of the book. People develop, and society takes great care in how it structures its citizens. As far as women are concerned, if our literature on them is a reflection of their 'estate' (their 'spirit' – a will to be free), this, according to Trilling, endangers the 'most intimate secret connection' which biology and culture have; it is of course one of the main points of the model presented in this book that this secret is uncoverable.

SU27

> As she says this there is a tremendous flash of lightning and peal of thunder. The ugly Beast becomes a most handsome

prince standing beside Beauty. The Beast thanks Beauty for
breaking a witch's spell.

Level of affect-signified: the Beast's transformation signifies an
affect of relief; mainly for the Beast but also for Beauty.

Level of grammatical unit: the third part of a three-part episode.

Level of results: this is entirely an inter-textual result and for an
important reason. By using the network of other texts that make
up the child's reading experience this story conceals its cunningness
over the humanisation and association with the father – the Beast
becoming a man is put down to magic, *not language*. The vital
thing about a conspiracy is that it should be left hidden.

Level of propositions: an active dramatic structure.

Level of signifiers: a new case value has to be added here which
is something like scenery and special effects; the agency for all this
is the fairy tale genre; it is obviously important that the Beast is
transformed.

Level of semiosis: the message here is quite clear: 'Beauty is
rewarded for being kind to the Beast; he becomes a man.' The code
here is the moral responsibility code; the message is something like:
'This is Beauty's reward for making amends'; the rule: guilt pays.

SU28

Next day, the Prince sent for her father, sisters and brothers.
He tells them that she promises to marry him. There is a grand
wedding at the castle with many guests. They live happily ever
after.

Level of affect-signified: a full type of security.

Level of grammatical unit: this is an ending and it recalls the
introduction.

Level of results: it is a cultural result that you tell the family of
the girl that you intend to marry her. The wedding is a completion
result and also, of course, cultural. Living happily ever after is pure
inter-textuality.

Level of propositions: descriptive dramatic structure.

Level of signifiers: a straightforward case structure.

Level of semiosis: the first message is a reminder that the reader
has been involved in a fairy tale and the second message must be
that because of Beauty's kindness to the Beast *everyone* is happy.

2.3 Melissa's reconstruction: introduction

Melissa was interviewed in her bedroom, which contained her books. She was asked what her favourite fairy tale was, and she named *Beauty and the Beast*. The full interview appears in Appendix C.

The reconstructed narrative is handled in the same way as Text 1. Each signifying unit is differentiated as it signifies affect. But we run into problems straight away in that, for the most part, the linear reconstruction is affectless or flat.[5]

When Text 1 was analysed, its two dimensions were simultaneously present in that, quite simply, the text provided enough information about both its dimensions; it was, if you will, redundant. This was especially true, for example, with the 'double-edged' result. Text I took the reader slowly through and very little was left to chance as to what set of meanings it was communicating.

Now, on the other hand, we come face to face with the problem of Melissa's reconstruction and its status as a semiotic system. Appendix B shows the result of the application of the model onto the reconstruction. The most difficult problem encountered has been filling out the vertical dimension; in fact, how the child reader has made Text I coherent or intelligible is impossible to discover from just the linear reconstruction of the SUs.

The vertical dimension is only partially present in Text 2, because it *is* the child's thought. In other words, how the reader grasps Text 1 is only partially revealed in the reconstruction she presents; some of the processes by which she grasps the story will remain hidden. This is where the interview becomes important, for it is here that the child's associations and thoughts about the story reveal what she has brought to bear upon the structure of Text 1.

The problem can be seen as a methodological one. In effect, the question I am asking is: 'How is it possible for me to read her story in order to find out how she read Text 1?' The answer is twofold:

(1) We know the structure and function of a fairy tale; we know in fact how it makes itself readable and what contents it intends, i.e. the analysis of the SUs.

(2) We also know that the reader will bring something to the text

---

[5] This flatness could be the result of a process described by Anderson and Bower (1973). They showed how the recall of significant (high affect) words was linked to contextual (low affect) cues. Although this is probably part of the explanation, we will see later on that flat affect has a functional value on that other signifiers receive strong affect.

and that moreover reading will be in the form of a type of problem solving.

What she does bring to the text is that part of the child's imagination that has rendered Text 1 intelligible *for her*. The only way we can understand this is to take each SU of Text 2 in turn, but this time with two 'backdrops':

(1)   The existential circumstances of the reader as revealed by observation and interview, in relationship to,

(2)   the original text.

The reconstruction is incomplete, whereas Text 1 is full. Whereas Text 1 is the product – inter alia – of stable and traditional systems of signification, Text 2 is the product of a developing thought structure which, if it is to be understood at all, must be seen in the broader context of the reader. Therefore, the recomposition that is represented in Appendix B has been filled in using three dimensions:

(1)   Text 1 (i.e. the model of it),

(2)   Text 2 (i.e. the linear reconstruction),

(3)   The thought structure inferred from points 1 and 2 and the interview data. The reconstruction plus the interview is the representation.

As for my place in this system, the semiotic perspective that I adopted for Text 1 will now have to be combined with the social psychological, i.e. a new perspective psycho-semiotics.[6]

2.3.1   *Melissa's story*

SU1

The nicest daughter was Beauty and the other one, the sisters, were selfish and they always wanted to take jewels and nice dresses.

Level of affect-signified: without too much inferring it can be said that Melissa has the two main themes presented by Text 1 in the same SU; there is also the overriding atmosphere of a material security enjoyed by all. This notion is also supported in various places in the interview, especially at question 2 where the father's kindness and generosity are touched on by Melissa.

Level of grammatical unit – this is an introduction, although a lot of those signifiers we would expect are not included. Nevertheless, the SU has a sort of descriptiveness about it.

---

[6] This is, of course, a restatement of Figure 1.5 along with the idea that reading is the application of a frame of reference in order to 'naturalise' the text. The hope is that with the use of these three perspectives the type and process of naturalisation carried out by Melissa will become clear.

Level of results: nowhere is the problem of this analysis more striking than in this section. The results represent a level of interface between reader and text. My problem is to find out where she has gone in order to render Text 1 coherent and, to a certain extent, I myself need a directional indicator. From the interview at various times it seems clear that she has used the external:inter-textual result; but they are inter-textual with a certain significance. So, for example, to take just one, we have the 'slip' of 'one sister' revealing Melissa's reference to her reading experience to one of Cinderella's sisters and at the same time the association of Cinderella's father with Beauty's and, of course, Cinderella with Beauty. It seems that another story is being used to *fill in* the present story (and one assumes vice versa); on the other hand, it also seems that there is more to it than *just* another story as a reading aid – they are obviously related thematically and one could infer, justifiably, that *Cinderella* has been used to render the twin themes of selfishness v. selflessness intelligible, mainly because they are much more pronounced in that story than here. Because of this we could say that, for some reason which is not quite clear at the moment, these themes are *extremely* important to Melissa.

In general then the level of results section will try to ascertain how Melissa has gone about finding coherence for the SUs of Text 1.

Level of propositions: this dramatic structure is descriptive; Melissa gives Beauty and her sisters attributes.

Level of signifiers: integrating the whole SU are the signifiers, the most primary string of which is the 'slip'; 'and the other one'; it is difficult at this point to know whether we are dealing with an error or a genuine slip of the tongue which is significant. We shall see later on that the 'one' sister starts to take on a primariness that makes it hard to classify as a mistake. We can see here too the fact that she has omitted the father and the brothers from her introduction and the impression, at this SU, is simply of the rivalry between the sister(s) and Beauty.

Level of semiosis: this is the other major interface with the reader and again I must situate myself in the face of it.

In Text 1 it was relatively easy to formulate a code that structured the message that each SU contained; this was mainly because of the predominance of primary signifiers, the integrated nature of the SUs and the existence of stable sub-codes within language. Here, on the other hand: what possible rule can there be and hence what message?

The difficulty again is that, whereas Text 1 was an intact semiotic system, Text 2 is incomplete mainly because it is not intended to take part in a process of signification; Melissa is not telling a story in the same way as the 'conspiratorial' narrator is in Text 1;[7] it is a text of a different purpose very much like an exegesis, a making over of Text 1, a making of it for herself. This process will be underpinned in two ways:

(1)   by the individual's thought, and
(2)   its relationship to society's codes.

Although they are both related in that her structure is in-the-world, they are nevertheless, because of its development, more or less coincident.

So at the S-level of SU1 there are two messages: the first says that this is a fairy tale – this is a process of connotation made possible by the affect-signified level and coherent via the intertextual result.

This level reveals the reconstruction as a 'version' rather than an exegesis.

The second message says something like: these themes are very important to me especially in the context of another girl (female), i.e. the exegetical is more important here. I propose that the first message here is identical to the connotative process that was going on in Text 1. We have a second order of signification in that the affect-signifieds within the context of a narrative signify a fairy tale.

The second message is process of communication based upon codes which are part of the reader's thought structure plus the other evidence we have such as the omission of father and brothers and the addition of the 'one sister';[8] the coherence or directional indicator here is extremely interesting in that it is also the intertextual result. That is, we have the story of *Cinderella* which figures prominently; but the story of *Cinderella* and its characters relate to

---

[7] In general what I want to do is to discover what meaning she has grasped from Text 1 and secondly to see how codified it is.

As a consequence, two possible levels can be deciphered in the semiosis section: the first will relate to significations structured by the reader's thought processes and the second to the extent these have been structured by codes and sub-codes.

[8] It is very difficult to label this. We could say that 'one sister' is a subtraction rather than an addition which would then give the additional problem of why a sister was being left out along with why one was being given a special place. Both these questions will be faced below, but for now I would like to label all *extra* signs 'additions' mainly because they show the extent of the reader's contribution to the process of reading.

Melissa's problem concerning the twin themes in the context of another girl. The inter-textual result is used to give a context to the affect-signifieds but these affect-signifieds also exist in her circumstances and certainly must make up part of her predicament and the reason why she is reading the story.

If this is true (and I hope to corroborate her motivation more fully below) the addition of 'one sister' means that she has started to think about this story vis-à-vis her experience concerning the themes and context outside, but in relation to, the fairy tale content.

We can say, therefore, that there are two messages at the S-level. The first deals with the well-established code of fairy tales and the other deals with part of the reader's experience which, although given some context by the various fairy tales she has read, is still problematic. We can start to get an idea of how she structures this aspect of her experience from the way she has represented the introduction.

This also leads on to the fact that there is another result that has been used to make the introduction of Text 1 intelligible; this has to do with the fact that culturally children read fairy tales for the specific purpose, I assume, of solving problems. This introduction to Text 1 has been rendered intelligible by the reader recognising this as an artefact that contributes to a need and this particular result was referred to in the analysis of Text 1. We know introductions are vitally important because of their transitional nature; these themes and this context take place in another place. The link, however, between this place and the existential predicaments of the reader is not simply guaranteed by the processes mentioned above; we must also consider the fundamental axioms of reading – identification and projection. Rather than assume these, we can see from the interview that it is almost entirely permeated with data that point to a very strong identification by Melissa with Beauty combined with a tendency to project herself into Beauty's situations. For example, both she and Beauty are very 'nice' in that they do the washing up without grumbling (see 5,7); her favourite flower is a rose which she would like (see 28, 29) and she describes Beauty as having blue eyes when they are illustrated as brown – it is Melissa's eyes that are *blue*. There are many examples of identification and projection and it seems quite clear that this is a fact of the reading. From the point of view of the primary signifiers there is little question about the importance of Beauty. On the other hand, vis-à-vis message two, we must also consider the slip as a primary (string) of signifiers.

SU2
. . . and but one day there was a dreadful fire.

Level of affect-signified: the affect here is the insecurity caused by the fire. But again from the point of view of the reconstruction the affect is 'flat'. In any case it does begin the seesaw effect of affect in that SU1 was over-written with security.

Level of grammatical unit: this is an event integrated by the specific affect of insecurity.

Level of results: the main result here is the inter-textual which refers the reader to other stories. Basically, after the introduction something has to happen and, as we have seen from the 'lure' section of Text 1, the affect-signified is opposed to the preceding SU in part.

Level of propositions: a factual structure.

Level of signifiers: the most interesting signifiers here are 'and' and 'but' which I consider to be separable for the following reasons:

'And' seems to be very much in the paradigm of 'then', i.e. a connector of the narrative in time; the 'but' shows us that this SU is dissimilar to the last one. This is mainly of course on the level of affect-signified; this is one of the ways the reader has of signifying the opposition of affect. So 'and but' signifies contiguity on one level (the narrative progression) and discontinuity on another level (affect-signified); all this has been made coherent in the first place by the inter-textual result.

Level of semiosis: this level is taken up entirely with a social codification identical to the message intended in the same place in Text 1: sometimes in fairy tales terrible things happen.

SU3

and so somebody called to the man ... the ... um ... father;
and go on, um, a ship with cargoes.

Level of affect-signified: the reader has again kept to the original affect pattern; hope of security.

Level of grammatical unit: this is a transition; the man/father is being called away.

Level of results: again she has used an inter-textual result and the clue to this is in her narrative at the start of this SU, 'and so'; these can't really be split up and she is signalling here that she is telling a story with a certain continuity which stories have as an attribute.

Level of propositions: anticipatory.

Level of signifiers: and 'and so' seems to be fundamental, as it helps to integrate the results level; but we can see also that she has added an agent to the SU, 'somebody'; the story does not mention who tells the father about his ship with the cargoes; Melissa has rendered this SU intelligible by deducing that somebody called him. It also shows us that she has used another result, an external:logical one, in that, if you 'hear' some news then someone must tell you; a simple logic of communicational processes deduced using secondary processing from the notion that, in this context, the receiver must have a sender. There next follows a string 'the man ... the ... um ... Father'. This is the first time the father has appeared and it almost seems like he is an after-thought; it is also confusing here at this SU because we can see from the interview that 'Father' is her favourite character. This may have something to do with the fact that until now the story has referred to him as either the father or the merchant; what we can say is that the addition of 'um' the reader is bringing one of the story's very primary signifiers into her representation by allowing her to substitute the signifiers – father for man. It is, as it were, a transition not only at the grammatical level but also here at the signifiers.

On the other hand, the next 'um' operates in a different way in that it is more like a question to herself along the lines of: 'What happens next?' This 'um' seems much more like a mnemonic than a significant sign. (Although that does not mean to say that it is not in some way significant – just that it is not clear what it is.)

Level of semiosis: the first message here deals with the connotation from the affect-signified level that 'fairy tales offer a glimmer of hope.'

The second message goes something like: 'the man in the story is also a father.' This is based upon the substitution she makes of man for father. Support for this is also the fact that in Text 1 this is when the father asks the daughters what they want from the wealth that the cargoes would bring (i.e. a fatherly action). It also gets validity from two other sources. The first is the interview where the father is generally seen as kind and generous – 'He got what they wanted' (see 2, 3 and 61). The second area of support for this message is this SU's structural relationship with SUs 2 and 4.

SU4

   ... and the daughters ... when he ... the daughters has to do
all the cleaning and the washing up because they had to move
in a small, little cottage.

Level of affect-signified: we have here the familiar patterning of the 'lure' but, whereas the insecurity of Text 1 was in the context of the theft of the money by the captain, for Melissa the insecurity comes out of SU2 where it really belongs.

Level of grammatical unit: as such it requires an 'event' label.

Level of results: how has she made Text 1 coherent and how can we tell from her presentation of SU4?

The '... when he ...' string is fairly easy for it refers to the proposed leaving of the father and is, therefore, a completion result. The move into a small, little cottage is also a completion result from SU2's fire. On the other hand, Melissa seems to think that the *reasons* they have to do the cleaning and washing up is because they moved into a small cottage – there is no mention of the loss of wealth directly; it is only signified in the size of the house, which is strongly emphasised.

Level of propositions: the reader is stating certain things.

Level of signifiers: putting the SU together as a whole it seems reasonable to assume that she has mixed up the sequencing both within and between. Within, she realises that it is not only 'when he' (leaves) ..., that the daughters are forced to do the housework; between the important point is the way she attenuates SU2 making it much more significant than it is in Text 1 by placing it in SU4.

Importance is also signified in the emphasis she places on the size of the cottage signifying the loss of material security. She does the same thing, for different reasons, with the emphasis on 'cleaning and washing up' as opposed to 'cooking and cleaning'. We can see from the interview at certain points that 'doing the washing up' is extremely important to Melissa (See 5, 6, 7, 8, 12, 14).

Level of semiosis: the use of attenuation by mixing the sequence of Text 1 gives us a clue as to what message the reader has picked up from the story. It is clear that washing up in the house is an important aspect of Melissa's daily life and she makes a point of associating herself and Beauty as two girls who get on with their chores; 'She just did it.' Not only does Melissa not grumble, she actually asks her mother if she can do it! Inter-textually, too, both Cinderella and Snow White are characters who do the cleaning, and it is hard not to conclude that selfishness (not being nice) is connected with refusing to pull your own weight in household chores. Melissa's mother confirmed that it was part of their philosophy that little girls did chores that fitted in with sex-roles (making the beds was the example given) and that, according to the mother, Melissa's father is also intent upon her washing up and cleaning her bedroom.

The message here goes something like: 'Washing up without protest is being a nice girl.' This message is caught up with the reader's experience of having to do household chores that the parents consider to be suitable for her. She has given 'washing up' an inter-textual context, and it seems that *Beauty and the Beast* is also important for the reader in that selflessness and how to 'give' as a girl are associated with chores. Text 1 makes it quite obvious that the sisters' greed and vanity is manifested in their reluctance to help around the house; wanting nice clothes and jewels is also to complain about work. To this extent then we must add another result, internal:similarity, the grumbling sisters have already been marked as selfish.

This SU is an extremely good example of a social codification (little girls should do things like this) having structured the reader's experience – the sisters grumbled, but then again they[9] are selfish (i.e. not nice).

Melissa seems to be well on her way to recognising this as a social necessity or more correctly as a 'natural'[10] way of being; so what is signified on the affect-signified level in Text 1 as selfishness appears on the S-level of the representation as a connotation about a way of doing as a girl in society. We can see this as well in questions 35 and 36; with Beauty gone, they 'had' to do the washing up. However, the question of the brothers (who seem to do nothing at all) taking part in the 'feminine' chore of washing up is doubted by Melissa; this is true even though they were nice like Beauty, i.e. not selfish (see 33).

The evidence seems to converge upon the fact that her experience of washing up, etc. has been structured by a social code put forward jointly by her parents and fairy tales as the proper way of doing. Because of this it seems reasonable to assume that Melissa has used an external:cultural result to read this part of the story.

Between SU 4 and 5 there is a very long pause and we must consider whether she has simply forgotten the story sequence or whether this is a significant lapse. My position will be that this pause is significant for it is related to the last SU in that it indicates that she realises she has mixed up the sequence of the story with SU4 and in fact over-emphasised the importance of the washing up in the first part of the story. But the pause is also related to Text 1 in that, after the disappointment of the theft of the money incident, the story begins all over again with the arrival of the Beast himself. Consequently, it seems reasonable to have a pause here because structurally the first part of the 'lure' is over. We can see also that in terms of the 'lure' an important negative affect is omitted in the space of the pause; its silence 'contains' the

---

[9] Parental injunctions also play a role. Of course, it is simply that this story is yet another way of allowing Melissa to make sense of *why* she has to do the washing up in the household.

[10] This idea of a naturalisation of social forms of being is part of the 'conspiratorial' nature of codes and codifying. The structure and function of Text 1 makes this clear as does the work of Leach (1964) and especially that of Barthes (1973).

disappointment of the father (and the reader). In fact SU3's ships with cargoes is not completed at all; rather it is completed by the washing up that refers back to SU2. One cannot help but get the impression that the importance of the 'selflessness/washing up' association has caused the reader to end the narrative at its most significant juncture *for her*. Although Text 1 allows this, she has used this allowance in her own peculiar way; it is only by encouraging her to go on and to 'forget' for the moment 'washing up' and its meaning that she can start the story again.

SU5
I think he got a rose

Level of affect-signified: where one would assume the affect to be most powerful for the daughter/reader it is most flat; but this is only if we concentrate upon the linear reconstruction; in the interview, on the other hand, the affective power of the rose is very clear. The sequence of questions from 28 to 32 shows that on the level of affect signified by the rose in our culture Melissa knows about the code.

Level of grammatical unit: this is the first part of an episode.

Level of results: this relates to the cultural use of the rose but as the interview makes clear, she is also aware that the father is 'getting what Beauty wanted'; see in particular questions 2, 3, and 28 where she at once identifies with Beauty and projects herself into Beauty's position of wanting a rose. So it seems that she has rendered the original SU coherent by an internal completion result which is also related to the code, i.e. a double-edged result. It is also clear that she has used an internal:similarity result in that father got what 'they' (see 2) wanted. This refers to SU1.

Level of propositions: an action has taken place.

Level of signifiers: the 'I think' is simply a response to my urging her to remember. The case values are straightforward.

Level of semiosis: from the re-presentation we can say that she has got the message about fathers and daughters and their affection for each other. The taking of the rose to her teacher, even though female, indicates the use of the rose in the context of 'parental' figure which, when combined with the fact that he got what she wanted, signifies the reciprocal nature of the giving of a rose in our culture. We can say then the message here is: 'The father loves his daughter very much.' We can see that Melissa's experience surrounding 'roses' is highly codified by the rule and is, therefore, an example of a strong coincidence of 'codes' that is to say, the affection for her father and his for her (i.e. Melissa's perception of it) is intelligible or structured in the rules about roses manifested both in the text and in her life.

SU6
and he got into trouble with the Beast

Level of affect-signified: the affect here is quite simple: an insecurity caused by the 'getting' of the rose.

Level of grammatical unit: the second part of an episode opposed to the first part.

Level of results: 'getting into trouble' signifies that she has gone to her experience of the 'law and order code' to make the incident in Text 1 coherent. So this is an external: cultural result.

Level of propositions: once again an action is taking place.

Level of signifiers: the 'and' is a familiar device used by the reader to connect SUs. The expression 'got into trouble with' is idiomatic and is left in the intermediate analysis as such. The case values are straightforward.

Level of semiosis: the message here is in the code of law and order and goes something like: 'He stole the rose from the Beast.' Once again we can see the connotation from the affect-signified level established by the code.

SU7
and he asked her ... um ... him to let Beauty ... um come to him ... and so she ... um ... came

Level of affect-signified: although from the reconstruction the affect is again quite flat, there is an insecurity here. The interview indicates that Beauty coming to the Beast generates some insecurity. Question 19 contains attributes like 'powerful', 'horrible-ness', that are bestial possibilities. Most important is the insecurity because of separation referred to inter-textually; *The Miller's Daughter* is her second favourite story. (See Appendix C.)

Level of grammatical unit: a transition.

Level of results: this section is complicated because of the slip 'and he asked her'. I have called this an internal:future result[11] in that it seems in part to be the result of the Beast's offer of marriage which happens, in Text 1, much later. We can also see from the interview that inter-textually the 'giving of daughters' is a primary theme in both *Rapunzel* and *The Miller's Daughter*. Beauty's arrival is an internal:completion result.

---

[11] An obvious contradiction in terms but it captures the 'foreshadowing' that goes on.

Level of propositions: action.

Level of signifiers: the slip of 'her' relates to the marriage proposal that happens later on in the story. But this is interesting vis-à-vis Text 1 which contains the message about what the Beast wants with 'one' daughter; the reader answers this question without waiting to build up suspense, all at once.

The first 'um' here works in much the same way as the 'um' in SU3. The reader substitutes him for her and the next two 'um's' seem also like the mnemonic 'um' in SU3.

Level of semiosis: SU7 is an important place in the reconstruction from the point of view of the meaning that the child is getting from Text 1.

At one level we can see that the reader fails to keep the suspense sanctioned by the problem-solving code in SU8, Text 1, so in a sense we can say that the reader has picked up on the question the story was posing at its S-level. But this is also the first time that the three main characters have appeared in a dramatic situation together and the substitutive 'um' allows us to see that, for the reader, Beauty and her father belong to the same paradigm and are in fact *inseparable*, in the first instance, from each other. This is the message then that rests upon the insecurity of separation signified in this SU: 'The father and daughter are inseparable.' Support for this comes from the interview in questions 24 to 28 where the closeness of the two is quite marked.

With 28 we can see the return of the 'one' sister who can now no longer be considered a mistake, '... *she* said it was ridiculous.' It seems pretty clear that Melissa is attaching quite a lot of blame for the separation of daughter and father on the one sister, '... he didn't want her to go' and '... I felt sorry for him,' (and finally) ... 'maybe she (Beauty) didn't want to go' (27).

But we know from the original text that the real blame lies at the feet of Beauty in a logical way: if she had not asked for the rose then father would not have 'got into trouble' with the Beast. On the other hand, although the sisters are quite right (for Melissa *the* sister), the reader exerts a righteous indignation, '... but I thought it was all right, I'd like a rose,' which can only be sanctioned socially, i.e. by the code of roses in the context of daughter and father; 'all right' can be read as 'socially acceptable'. We can see that in question 32 it is 'all right' to give the rose to the teacher, even though one is not allowed to pick them oneself (Melissa's father is the family gardener); one supposes that picking roses oneself would 'get you into trouble'. The overall impression is of a shifting of the blame for the father's predicament which is itself defused. The real affect here: the separation anxiety and sense of responsibility for the dilemma are drained from the linear reconstruction and *displaced in the interview* from Beauty to the 'one' sister or, from the reader's point of view, *from Melissa to whomever this 'one' sister is* in her situation.

This multi-functional SU faces not only to the paradigmatic similarity but also to the future and, on the way, cuts out the suspense of the story[12] by answering the questions posed by Text 1. On the other hand, we can see from the interview data that this SU is fleshed out by Melissa around the signifier of 'one sister'; i.e. the implications of the story at this point centre around the sister and the desire Melissa has to 'make sense of her': this results in a further message that 'the father and daughter are separated by the sister.'

This two part message is a good example of where Melissa's experiencing of the story is well structured by codes – the rose and the father/daughter – and also where codes cannot bind the reader's experience because a particular signifier is too important to the reader, i.e. the one sister. The continual use of this sister shows an idiosyncratic primary processing, at the same time using, of course, the context of the story's other signifiers.

From the point of view of the 'lesson' the story has already led the reader to associate this sister with extreme selfishness, very unlike Beauty (and, therefore, Melissa), yet it remains, at this point, unclear as to whether the essential lesson, a girl's selflessness faced with a man's desires, is being interiorised.

We can, however, see something of the primary structure of Melissa's thought centred as it is around the selfishness (not nice) and Father. The idea of being 'nice' is processed by Melissa, in this context, as a girl helping around the house unlike the 'one' sister. What is missing of course from this chain of signifiers is 'marry' and one of the functions of this SU has been to 'include it out'.

The importance of this SU in the interpretive process from my perspective is unmistakable: a lot of affect is 'crunched' into this SU. We can see too the processes used and the particular way Melissa makes sense out of this part of the story, her ability to grasp the social themes and at the same time to flesh out, as part of the task of reading, the implications of the text for her.

---

[12] It could be argued, I suppose, that there is little chance of a suspenseful reconstruction because she has read this before and many times. This would be to miss the point of the 'favourite' story; the reader 'lives' Beauty's situations and the interview makes this abundantly clear. It is also to confuse re-presentation with recall; the reader is *making* sense out of this story for herself, not testing her powers of remembering.

SU8

But she broke a promise when she saw her father ill and she
said she'd come back after two months but she didn't.

Level of affect-signified: the affects here are selfishness, where
Beauty's breaking of the promise is combined with the father's
illness. In terms of the affect-signifieds this linking of Beauty's
behaviour with her father's illness serves the function of lessening
the selfishness signified. Text 1 after all proposed the selfish act
after the father had recovered; Melissa proposes it contiguously
with the father's illness. It is interesting to note that this lessening
of affect seen here is the heightening of affect seen in SU1 where
the twin themes were given special emphasis through the inter-
textual result (see the use of the 'sister' *Cinderella*) and it seems
that this is one of the processes of reading; the intensity of affect
can be manipulated by the reader for comprehension.

Level of grammatical unit: this is an event because of the specificity of affect (even though reduced in intensity).

Level of results: we can say with some certainty that breaking
the promise and the terms of it (2 months, etc) have been rendered
coherent because of her father's illness. This would be then an
external:cultural result based upon the affection (duty) of daughters
for fathers; this accounts for the lessening of the affect-signified.

Level of propositions: the overall impression is that Melissa is
stating information.

Level of signifiers: 'but' is a significant conjunction here, it allows
Melissa to contain the idea that Beauty went home in the first place
in order to break the promise. Until now the analysis of SU8 has
not been able to tell us where Beauty's behaviour takes place. The
use of 'but' at one level indicates an opposition of situation; it
could be expanded to say 'but she did not stay with the Beast.'

Similarly 'but' plays another role in which it introduces a
complex reconstruction based around the case values of time and
location.[13] This SU signifies a certain diluted affect through the
manipulation of contexts. We know she broke her promise at her
home but Melissa would have it that Beauty broke it *when* she saw the
ill father. This really takes place in the palace as does in fact
her promising to come back in two months; on the other hand 'but
she didn't' is located at her home. This mixing of the time and location of acts in the story is an important part of her reconstruction

---

[13] Although no location value is given in Appendix B, SU8, it
can be seen as an 'understood' case; events must take place somewhere. It is, however, true that 'location' is significant here because
it is not mentioned which contributes to its grammatical function.

for two reasons:

(1) It allows her to integrate this SU so that it signifies a lessened affect of selfishness (Beauty/Melissa are not selfish; it is the sister(s) who are) and continues a process of displacement of the responsibility that we saw quite clearly in SU7, where *the* sister comes in for the blame.

(2) Grammatically she contains the movement of the story in a static event and so what is stated as mere information in the reconstruction is in fact significant in the story, especially the mixed feelings the story is trying to create concerning the Beast and his humanity – in effect his prospect as a groom. This facilitates the process of omission; the vital absence being the Beast's sadness at letting Beauty return home and his warning of what would happen if she broke her promise.

Level of semiosis: when we come to the meaning that the child is taking from this part of the story, it is a connotation arising from the weakened selfishness: 'Beauty breaks the promise because of her father's illness'; in fact, for Melissa there are mitigating circumstances. We have a certain support for this in the interview at questions 26 and 27 where Melissa ventures the idea that they did not really want to be apart in the first place (although she changes her mind after the transformation of the Beast, see 39).

So even though Beauty has wronged in breaking a promise, the whole SU goes up to make it not such a great crime. The code structuring this is the father/daughter code and a drained affect of selfishness is necessary for this message.

In many ways this SU rejects the possible metaphorical substitution of Beast for father. In the original story we have seen how the Beast and the father are related through affect and Beauty's reactions. Melissa condenses all this and creates a metonymy (I) which distorts just when and where she breaks her promise; the association is with Beauty and her father which follows from the inseparability mentioned in the last SU and continues here. The interview brings this out at question 17 where she is stuck for another character as her favourite. This is also the case at question 23. On the other hand, it seems clear that when she is probed about the Beast, 18–21 for example, she has a representation of him and his relationship with Beauty, '. . . he didn't . . . he wasn't horrible to Beauty.' Is this representation of the Beast part of the same network of association as the father? The nearest she does come to associating the two is through the relationship between the signifiers, 'cruel' (see 3), 'powerful' and 'horrible' (see 19). Furthermore the opposite of 'horrible' seems to be 'nice' (19) and one of the meanings given to nice is 'selflessness'; the Beast was not selfish with Beauty, but then neither was the father. It seems that the only other person who is selfish is the 'one' sister who received this affect within the context of 'household chores' and as the person responsible for the father's/Beauty's predicament – it was 'all right to ask for a rose'.

In general the meaning being 'grasped' in these last two SUs has to do with 'mitigating' circumstances; i.e. displacement. In SU7 the sister was at fault; in this SU Beauty's breaking of the code of 'promise keeping' is displaced onto the father's illness (the father/daughter code) and I have shown how she does this through a metonymy that mixes up the dramatic structure, especially time and location. Finally once again we can see the blurring of the distinction of S-level messages in that here there is a strong coincidence of codes. The mitigating circumstances also relate to Melissa's feelings for *her* father and they are insinuated into the representation because of these feelings – why else put them in?

SU9

... and so um she dreamed that she saw um Beast um dead under a large tree and when she went there she did and then there was thunder and he woke up.

Level of affect-signified: where we would expect guilt through the making amends, especially agreeing to marry and declaring love for the Beast, we find instead excitement. Furthermore, this is the first time in the re-presentation that an affect-signified is found solely in the interview, primarily at question 20, but, as I will show below, made coherent within the structure by other questions, see questions 55, 58.

There is also an overriding insecurity here that must be part of the excitement that Melissa feels when reading this part of the story; the Beast is dead and then 'wakes up'; Beauty has to go to him and the thunder and lightning constitute a 'good scene', see question 58.

Level of grammatical unit: she has managed to combine here an episode and a transition; the reason that these are in one SU is because of the affect of excitement that is signified. In fact this is an event because of the affect, but it is very difficult to classify because it is not really specific – the excitement is diffuse and contains many components. In any case we can say that vis-à-vis Text 1 so much is drained out of the original that Melissa more or less *states* what has happened. Because of this I would like to say that this is probably best classified as an Event.

Level of results: this level starts to give some clue as to what it is that excites Melissa about this part of the story. Through the use of external:inter-textual results Melissa fills in gaps that are not so much part of Text 1's structure (I have shown how 'neat' this is) but Melissa's *perception* of these holes.

The scenes that Melissa is reading are structured in the first instance by the fairy tale code through the inter-textual result. We have especially here both *Rapunzel* and *The Miller's Daughter* which fall within the code. But on the other hand even though they fall within the fairy-tale code and are good examples of it (the selfish witch and the magical transformation of hay into gold) what Melissa actually uses them for vis-à-vis how she fills in her con-structed gaps is much more idiosyncratic and 'asocial' than the code.

From the context of the fairy-tale code *Rapunzel* is the main story that she uses but her second favourite story, *The Miller's Daughter*, is used as well; both will be discussed in the semiosis section. It is probably a safe inference that she has used an internal: completion result as well – the string 'and so' seems to indicate this.

Level of propositions: the overall dramatic structure is factual although what is stated is active.

Level of signifiers: 'and so . . .' as mentioned above is one of the ways that Melissa signifies the completion of a previous action, see SU7. This conjunction, though, is slightly more of a 'therefore' than that in SU7 in that it is the result of breaking the promise; it is much more definite, given the code surrounding 'promises'.

The 'ums' here seem to have the function of de-affecting the unit; after all Beauty is going through a lot of agonising in this part of Text 1. The 'ums' seem negatively mnemonic, simply allowing her to get onto those aspects that she desires to reconstruct and which also allow her to remain coherent.

The primary signifiers in this SU are the 'and she did' and 'he woke up'. The first represents an enormous simplification. What seems to have happened is that she would rather not reconstruct this part of the story. Question 55 makes it pretty certain that she knows what happened and that the declarations of love and marriage are the cause of embarrassed laughter. The Beast's beastification and transformation into a prince is elaborated in the interview by the inter-textual experience, i.e. *Rapunzel*. The ques-tion is: what is it about *Rapunzel* and, for that matter, her other fairy tales that make sense out of this part of Text 1?

Level of semiosis: we have here, I think, at this moment of her greatest excitement in reading the story her most important state-ment of the solution she has imposed upon the structure offered to her. We also have the explanation as to why she is excited. The expression 'she did' is a displacement. We have seen this process before in Melissa's reconstruction and what she *is* consistent about is who receives the negative affect that the text has tried to signify (and, in fact, through its own conspiratorial process get the reader to accept): that person is the 'one' sister.

Fitting *Rapunzel* into all this is very interesting from the point of view of the model of reading; the inter-textual result leads to a particular area of experience which has been structured by the fairy-tale code; in this case the code structures the 'transformation' of characters. In *Rapunzel* the prince is made blind (not by the witch as Melissa would have it but because of a fall when he thinks Rapunzel is dead) then transformed back into a prince and they live happily ever after. There is a fairly concrete rule in the fairy-tale code that says that people – and characters generally – can be changed and changed back again. So we have at a very coded level the message: 'This is a fairy tale.'

Why does she consider *Rapunzel* to be a good token of the code? The answer is that there are other attributes of this story that make Melissa's understanding of *Beauty and the Beast* coherent for her. *Rapunzel* is about the 'giving of a child' and so is *Beauty and the Beast*; the difference is that whereas in *Beauty and the Beast* it is the Beast who is receiving the child; in *Rapunzel* it is the witch. Both the Beast and the witch covet and keep the daughters; but whereas the Beast becomes steadily humanized, the witch remains evil, jealous and vindictive right to the end. The stories are similar in that it is the daughters who 'break the spell'; in *Rapunzel* her tears make the prince see again (he 'wakes up'). In our text we know that it is Beauty and her love of the Beast that make him 'wake up'. The difference is that there is no spell in *Rapunzel* but there is (or was in the past) in *Beauty and the Beast*.

Now we can 'enter into' Melissa's solution and the problem she is solving here where the difference makes a difference. *Rapunzel* is distorted by Melissa (i.e. she puts a spell into that story) in order to realise the primary difference which is the fact that whereas Beauty has no *mother*, Rapunzel *does* in the form of the jealous stepmother.

We do not have to go far to understand this: in Text 1 we saw that the mother was significant because of her absence – 'mother would have got in the way' and for Melissa she is quite definitely no longer part of the mother-father-family paradigm – 'she's dead,' see question 60. Furthermore, from the interview the inter-textual clues are very strong in favour of the significance of the mother as this 'one' sister that is constantly referred to by Melissa. *Snow White* is used because of the jealous and evil queen who just happens to desire to be the most 'beautiful'; although 'she hasn't got two sisters' she has got what Beauty hasn't got and Melissa does have, a mother. So in fact does Cinderella, '... a wicked sort of mother, but she (Beauty) hasn't got one you see' (question 12). All the stories, including her 'second favourite', contain what the 'authors' of *Beauty and the Beast* felt obliged to leave out. Not only does Melissa reinstitute the mother back into the family through the inter-textuality but also through the 'one' sister who is greedy, vindictive and does not care for Beauty very much.[14]

Text 1 had to leave the mother out because of its messages concerning 'men-selflessness-guilt', etc., but Melissa has to have her included.

The reason for this is simply that in the context of the story of *Beauty and the Beast* within the structure that it has and within the context of the reader's life – her existential predicament – *mother* needs to be understood; she is part of her thought at this moment which she wants to have structured for her. The relevance of *Beauty and the Beast* is that it attempts this with the affective context of selflessness v. selfishness; furthermore it links this very often with the primary affective contradiction: security v. insecurity.

Now we know for certain that, in Melissa's family, being selfless takes the form (there are probably many others) of doing the household chores; not only that but they are the chores that 'women' should do (Snow White washed up at the dwarf's house). It seems clear that the contradiction that Melissa feels is structured and has *been* structured around the selflessness v. selfishness and that the mediator is the 'one' sister who, in Melissa's context, must be the mother.

But this is a displacement in that it is much easier for Melissa to unload this negative affect on a sister than on a parent; all the bad feelings, the greed, the ridicule and the grumbling are associated with this one sister who is once removed from mother and twice removed from the centre of these feelings, Melissa herself. We can see that she does this for two reasons:

(1) Melissa knows that she too is selfish; in question 65 she is the one with the most clothes in the family, and
(2) It seems a reasonable inference that she would feel selfish if she did not wash up in her house. This is obviously how her family gets her to do things; by making her feel selfish they present the possibility of a withdrawal of love or security; no one loves a bad girl, one who is not nice. For Melissa, rather than

---

[14] In the *Introductory Lectures* (1974) Freud makes a similar point in discussing the arrival of a brother or sister and the incumbant's reaction: 'It is even true that as a rule children are far readier to give verbal expression to these feelings of hate than those that arise from the parental complex' (p. 377).

contain this, she projects bad feelings onto the mother. As a consequence she surpasses these feelings (momentarily), and the solution takes on what Dunker (1972) would have called a functional value.

Also this same feeling she has is related to her relationship with her father; not only is her father, according to the mother, keen on her doing female chores, but he is also clearly adored by his daughter (see 61). However, whereas in Text 1 Beauty and her father were extremely close (she was his pet), this relationship in Melissa's family is impossible, mainly for the reasons that it was possible in the story – the mother. It is the mother who separates father and daughter (SU7) just as it must be the case in Melissa's family. So once again in a different yet related context, the mother mediates these feelings for Melissa. She is both selfish with husband (father) who sides with her in the household chores problem – and selfless in that as her mother she cannot be all bad.

Beauty and the Beast provides an almost perfect mirror for the child; what it lacks, and must lack, is a mother; Melissa fills in the gap that she perceives in the text. This is her favourite because the contradiction that Melissa feels between her selfishness (she has the most dresses) and her selflessness (she asks mother if she can do the washing up) is within the context of female duties that are being thrust upon her in the process of feminisation and also within the context of her relationship to her father and mother. The displacement of the affects onto the mother/sister as mediator momentarily resolves this feeling but it can never be a final solution. For underlying all this is, of course, the primary contradiction which permeates the use made of the two secondary affects. Selfishness, she has been taught, leads to insecurity, a withdrawal of love and consequently a sense of guilt; selflessness on the other hand leads to security, love, recognition, etc. Faced with this, Melissa, in real life, has little choice but to situate herself, if she wants recognition, closer to the 'nice' girl position than the bad. This means doing certain things like washing up. But we know too that the text had other 'things' in mind, the switching of her desire from father to another man motivated by guilt. Melissa's lesson was to be that she would be living one day within the context of 'other' household chores burdened by a sense of guilt. Up to now the process of uncovering the reader's reading has been based upon the model and its system; that is to say the inferences have been tied down. When we come to that area of her thought containing herself, father, mother, selflessness and guilt, all the interview reveals is an embarrassed laugh and an 'I don't know.'

This is obviously a denial of the facts of the story concerning marriage and love and guilt. What must be asked is: how far do the data support the notion that Melissa has interiorised the lesson? There are two pieces of evidence directly related to this: the first is the nervous laugh when she is asked, in a more direct way than usual, about the final interaction between Beauty and the Beast. Her denial, 'I don't know ...' combined with the laugh indicates that she *does* know, or has a fairly good idea.

The second piece of evidence comes from her second 'favourite' tale (see questions 57, 58). This story is also about the 'giving of children' but her answer in 58 allows an interpretation that seems to indicate a further denial of the story's lesson and that, in fact, although she may have it, she does not feel ready for it.

There are two points to be made at 58:

(1) It seems clear that she has made a strong identification with the Miller's daughter: she tells us as much in the slip 'I haven't' and her correction of it, '... and she says ...'.

(2) The next slip is very important. Melissa says that Rumpelstiltskin asks the Miller's daughter for her children 'when you grow up' but the Miller's daughter is not a little girl – she is very marriageable and is, in fact, married to the King three days after meeting him and they soon have a baby. It is in fact Melissa who is the little girl that will have to grow up, get married and have babies. I would argue that Melissa does not *feel* herself to be ready for that now.

The Miller's Daughter is significant for the solution as indeed are the other texts. *Cinderella*, *Snow White* and *Rapunzel* share one important thing in common: they contain wicked mothers! *The Miller's Daughter* does not; rather it contains a good mother who loves and cherishes her baby, '... but she didn't want to give her young'. Once again the emphasis is on the mother but this time she is good, just like Melissa will be when she grows up. What constitutes a good wife/woman/mother is what Melissa has to learn, and *Beauty and the Beast* is one way of positioning the reader in this problem.

With this analysis of Melissa's solution the thesis reaches its limit best signified perhaps by the embarrassed laugh. The point is that although the evidence indicates that she has denied the lesson this does not mean that this structure has not been packed away for future use *when she is grown up*.

What I can do is to point to the evidence that is all around the 'laugh' and add that it should be remembered that Melissa is in a process of *becoming* and trying to make sense out of her feelings and the world. The primary signifier for her is the 'one' sister, the analysis of which has shown its importance in the re-presentation and Melissa's life at the moment. She is reading the story to 'get' the one sister, i.e. to understand her in the context of family life.

The last point accounts for the excitement that Melissa feels which she would rather put down to 'it's just a good scene.' What *is* exciting is that she has been allowed by the text to explore the meaning of mother. Put another way, she is exploring the code that will enable her to understand herself in relation to mother and father and *this is exciting*.

This is not to deny the entertainment that is going on (the thunder, lightning and transformation, etc.), it is to point out that through the entertainment the child is allowed to explore or 'flesh out' the meaning of mother and, in this case, females (herself) generally. There can be no greater excitement than being allowed to make what is inarticulate, confusing and unstructured, clear. However, the price of this is her 'feminisation' in other areas such as doing the washing up.

As for the meaning grasped here, it is very difficult to summarise because we have in SU9 the culmination of the solution imposed. She rejects, or refuses to enunciate, the switch of feelings from father to Beast and instead wishes to situate mother in the relationship; this seems to me a wholly realistic type of solution. The message gained from the reading could be summed up, perhaps inadequately as: 'I love my father but my mother is a problem!'

What is missing here is the fact that the affective contradiction is Melissa's and that the mother is the 'surplus signifier' that mediated it; so selflessness and selfishness are contained by mother who ultimately contains the primary affects because of the way these two secondary affects are related to them.

SU10
... and they had a wedding

Level of affect-signified: the happiness here is quite genuine; she is happy for Beauty, the Beast and the father because 'he wanted her to get married' (see 39).

Level of grammatical unit: an ending which is much like an event.

Level of results: all the other fairy tales used have a happy ending therefore we have an inter-textual result and there is also a completion result: 'She wakes up.'

Level of signifiers: 'and' indicates a completion; 'they' does not include, for Melissa, the sisters, see 51.

Level of semiosis: the reading of the story could be said to have ended in SU9; SU10 is really a very classical dénouement but significantly Melissa would like to emphasise the rapproachement with the sisters (I am assuming especially the 'one' sister) which *does* happen in the story but which, I think, Melissa does not quite believe (see question 51).

In fact, this supports the analysis in SU9; the problem with mother (and herself) is never solved; only mediated. So the happiness signified here is only partial; she would really like once and for all to be at one with her mother – but in her 'existential predicament' this is, at the moment, impossible. Thus the message here is that the situation is not entirely happy and also the fairy tale message is not far away in either this SU or the last.

By way of summary we can say that whereas Bettelheim would suggest the text offers 'subtle solutions' to affect problems, what the reader does with these 'solutions' (in this case the switching of feelings) is largely the result of the person reading the text. We cannot say for sure that the lesson has not been interiorised as a structure to be used later on, but I have tried to point out how the developing reader is caught up in a process of structuring which offers her the chance to think in a particular way.

2.4 Conclusions and discussion

In this last section I want to summarise some of the gains that have been made, i.e. what has been learnt about texts and reading. I also want to situate the work within the general academic problematics of psychology and semiotics and state more clearly the case mentioned above for a psycho-semiotics. Finally, I want to outline the methods used so that the presented analyses can be carried out by interested readers on, not only other children's literature, but perhaps on other semiotic systems with other psychological readers.

2.4.1 *On reading*

It seems clear now to me that reading can be seen as a type of problem solving along the lines of the emotional problem solving originally posed by Bettleheim (1978). However, the process is not as simple as Bettleheim made out; the overriding process is what I have called 'naturalisation', a term borrowed from poetics. What I have shown is that, in the case of fairy tales, this process of naturalisation is directed by the story and in fact it is a 'conspiratorial' goal of the text to direct the reader to 'natural' ways of thinking about their problems. The important point is, of course, that these ways of thinking and being proposed by the text are not natural at all but social and accepted and thus 'necessary'.

The process is carried out by filling in of the text. What is filled in is a perceived lack or need in the text that is also felt by the reader, i.e. there is an affective structure in the text that is relevant to the reader's life.

This structure is based in the two primary affects of security and insecurity. Structure, however, is not enough, for it is important that a relevant contact also be presented in the text for it is primary signifiers, surplus signifiers, which are the vehicles of this process.

Reading vis-à-vis the structure of the text is extremely selfish; Melissa needs to come to terms with her mother and father. The text offers a structure which is rich in signification both at the level of affect and semiosis but the potential of the text to signify negative affect is from the analysis presented reduced and flattened; the guilt intended for Melissa ends up at the feet of the sister. It is not a case of children reading 'because they like to be frightened' but rather in order to find out about important problems they are faced with as they grow up; cultural artefacts lodge the answers in insecurity. The most important process that gets the child through such stories is displacement of affect onto a signifier that is well positioned to take up the surplus affect. This use of the text is extremely clever; the main point of *Beauty and the Beast* was to direct the reader to thinking about the Beast, marriage, guilt and herself, but the reader uses the story to think about her mother – she postpones the grim reality she will one day face, she stays as a child attached to her father and finding every reason to distrust her mother. The important point is that at the centre of reading seems to be but one primary signifier, mediating primary affects, satisfying desires and central to an enormous network of signifiers whose connections are more or less directed by codes, and whose implications the child will explore in a more or less directed way to make the text intelligible.

We can see, too, how the process of reading is underpinned by language itself, in that any thought about signifiers is possible because of the twin poles of language metaphor and metonymy. Investigating meaning by exploring (Empson) one's chains of signification (Lacan) is a process of selection of signifiers and fleshing out the wholes which form their contexts. The one sister is both metaphorical, a selection, and metonymical, part of a context, which if she could explore it fully would eventually lead to attaching negative affects to signifiers which would cause great distress, viz. either her mother or herself. Instead the affect is displaced onto the surplus signifier.

We could state this from the point of view of literary criticism. The reader re-writes the text, 'foregrounding' that which is central to her thought and backgrounding that which is unwelcome to her thought. If this is true then the background is there and there is good reason to assume that this background, at another point in time, could be foregrounded. The notion as to whether structures which the code has tried to create are totally lost or are simply packed away for future reference cannot be shown here but it still remains a very good possibility given the reader's involvement in her favourite fairy tale. Again, this involvement is axiomatically based in the processes of identification and projection; the reader is identifying with the heroine situated in a particular structure with a particular content.

2.4.2   *On the text*

We have seen how the text is a coherent, integrated structure that depends upon the dramatic structure of language. The goal that I set at the beginning was to uncover what the child was faced with and my answer is a semiotic system with social psychological intentions.

As a semiotic system it depends upon the twin poles of language. It offers through its structure the possibility of significations being transformed from the text (type I) to the world of the reader (type II). It articulates a particular world for the reader by proposing metaphors and metonymies which are socially and psychologically acceptable.

The text is a coherent structure which offers directional indicators on where to go to find its coherence, either in the text itself or externally in the reader's experience. Most importantly, the text has an affect structure which is an integral, inseparable part of its semiotic function.

The text grammar shows that the fairy tales considered are also literary facts which have a macro structure that attracts the reader and then teaches the reader but we have also seen how this and indeed all other levels are integrated, speak with one voice as it were; they are all marshalled for its conspiratorial intentions.

2.4.3   *Psychology and semiotics*

One of my goals was to show how any signification could be grasped from the text. If the reader is Bettelheim, then an extremely well worked out thought structure is brought to bear upon the story, i.e. the meta-psychological framework of psycho-analysis especially that which deals with the Oedipus complex.

It seems clear though that Bettelheim's is a 'second' reading; his involvement is different from the identifying child reader 'living' Beauty's predicaments. Even so I would argue that both readings, hers and Bettelheim's, are accounted for by the range of meaning that the text grammar demonstrates is possible. The difference between the readings has to be located in the signifying chains each has explored in order to render the text intelligible, the framework brought to bear upon the text.

The important point to be answered is where is the reader when reading? The semiotician would attempt to offer a theory of reading by describing all the systems of signification within a text but without or outside the reader who is 'only a methodological necessity'. The book has shown that reading is a psychological process and that the person is at a particular place in the signifying chains at a particular time. The semiotician attempts to map the entire field – the whole structure which is all the codes and sub-codes. There is never any attempt to study how the codes are used and produced. Without this there is no notion of reading, no subject with no development and no emotions. Codes, like history, are produced from what I have termed here, after Bettelheim, existential predicaments; as such they are only independent to the extent that the users are, theoretically (cf. also Lévi-Strauss) negated from the process. This becomes apparent when the reader reads her favourite fairy tale in an attempt to solve a problem that is real enough both internally and externally for the reader; the process of development that this reveals is an active making sense out of the environment and its institutions. People produce the codes.

2.4.4   *Method*

The method can be divided into two parts. The first deals with the informant and the second deals with the texts (1 and 2).

The methods in the first part owe a lot to in depth interviewing techniques and general ethnographic procedure. This must always be combined though with a certain experience and intuition, especially about primary signifiers, which is very like the key-word analysis proposed by Evans-Pritchard (1951).[15] Above all one must listen to the informant and be sensitive to where she wants to go and does not want to go. The reader can also be asked to draw the

---

[15] '... The most difficult task in anthropological field work is to determine the meaning of a few key words upon an understanding of which the success of the whole investigation depends' (p. 80). This could be the task of 'understanding the personality as well: what is the patient's key sign?'

story or parts of it. All the verbal data are recorded and transcribed.

In many ways the advice of the anthropologist Clifford Goertz who recommends *An Enthnography of the Disciplines* (1979) seems valuable. That is to treat one's subject matter, in this case the child's version of a favourite fairy tale and associations to it, as an exotic language, from an exotic culture – first one must understand the language and how to use it. A photocopy of the text is taken.

The methods used for the text are as follows:

After Lévi-Strauss, the text is broken down into a minimal set of sentences and, after Bettelheim, the criterion for this is the extent to which they signify affect; these are the SUs. Next carry out an intermediate case analysis in order to clarify the original decomposition and to demarcate the grammatical units, results and the case values for the signifiers which allows a propositional description in terms of dramatic structure.

The SUs are then recomposed using the rule of integration. The notion of connotation and primary signifier is used to establish the S-level of message and code. The same procedure is used for both texts except that for Text 2 there are two different S-level messages possible.

Also, through the method of 'convergent validation', the solution that the reader has imposed is sought from the representation and observation, i.e. all available sources. The solution should come to light as the only possible mediation of an affective contradiction that has already been established in the first textual analysis.

Deciphering the solution will be helped if one is guided by Raymond Chandler's maxim:

> There are things that are facts, in a statistical sense, on a tape
> recorder, in evidence. And there are things that are facts
> because they have to be facts, because nothing makes any sense
> otherwise. (1958, p. 132)

Appendix A
Signifying Units of the Text
of Beauty and the Beast

1

SIGNIFYING UNIT	Once upon a time there lived a rich merchant in a beautiful house with lovely gardens. He had four sons and three daughters. The two eldest, Miranda and Rosina, were vain and lazy. They liked satin dresses and jewels. The youngest was Beauty who was her father's pet. She was industrious, kind and loving to all.
LEVEL OF SEMIOSIS	This is a fairy tale
LEVEL OF GRAMMATICAL UNIT	Introduction
LEVEL OF AFFECT SIGNIFIED	Selfishness v. selflessness Security
LEVEL OF RESULTS	External: inter-textual External: cultural
LEVEL OF PROPOSITIONS	Descriptive

LEVEL OF SIGNIFIERS	*Once upon a time (T)	Rich (Att) Merchant (A)

Beautiful (att)
House (L)
Lovely (att)
Gardens (L)
He (A)
4 sons (att)
3 daughters (att)
2 eldest (att)
Miranda & Rosina (A)
Vain & Lazy (att)

Satin dresses (O)
Jewels (O)
Youngest (att)
Beauty (A)
Father's pet (att)
She (A)
Industrious (att)
Kind (att)
Loving (att)
To all (R)
lived
liked

2

SIGNIFYING UNIT	The merchant lost his palace in a fire and his ships in a storm. The family moved into a small cottage. The two vain daughters grumbled about cooking and cleaning and coarse clothes.	
LEVEL OF SEMIOSIS	Sometimes in fairy tales terrible things happen.	
LEVEL OF GRAMMATICAL UNIT	Event	
LEVEL OF AFFECT SIGNIFIED	Selfishness Insecurity	
LEVEL OF RESULTS	External: inter-textual External: cultural Internal: similarity	
LEVEL OF PROPOSITIONS	Factual	
LEVEL OF SIGNIFIERS	Merchant (R) Palace (O) *Fire (P) Ships (O) *Storm (P) Family (A) *Lost	Small (att) Moved Cottage (L) Grumbled 2 (att) Daughters (A)

Cooking (O)	Coarse (att)
Cleaning (O)	Clothes (O)

3

SIGNIFYING UNIT	One year later the merchant heard that one ship is safe. He prepared to travel to the ship to get the gold yielded by the cargo.
LEVEL OF SEMIOSIS	But fairy tales always leave a glimmer of hope
LEVEL OF GRAMMATICAL UNIT	Transition (I)
LEVEL OF AFFECT SIGNIFIED	Hope of security
LEVEL OF RESULTS	External: inter-textual External: logical Internal: similarity
LEVEL OF PROPOSITIONS	Anticipatory
LEVEL OF SIGNIFIERS	*One (att) to travel (P) Year later (T) Ship (L) Merchant (R) to get (P) One (att) Gold (O) Ship (O) *prepared *Safe (att) Cargo (O) He (A) heard yielded by

4

SIGNIFYING UNIT	The father asks the daughters what they want. Miranda wants dresses. Rosina wants jewels. Beauty wants her father's safety and a rose. He sets out.
LEVEL OF SEMIOSIS	Life could return to the introduction

LEVEL OF GRAMMATICAL UNIT	Transition (II)	
LEVEL OF AFFECT SIGNIFIED	Selfishness v. selflessness Security (material/affective)	
LEVEL OF RESULTS	Anticipatory Descriptive	
LEVEL OF SIGNIFIERS	Father (A)	*Father's (O)
	*Daughters (R)	*Safety (O)
	What they want (O)	*Rose (O)
	Miranda (A)	We (A)
	*Dresses (O)	asks
	Rosina (A)	wants
	*Jewels (O)	promises
	Beauty (A)	sets out

5

SIGNIFYING UNIT	He discovers that the captain has stolen the money. He is disappointed for the children.	
LEVEL OF SEMIOSIS	Remember the event	
LEVEL OF GRAMMATICAL UNIT	Event	
LEVEL OF AFFECT SIGNIFIED	Selfishness Insecurity	
LEVEL OF RESULTS	External: cultural Internal: similarity	
LEVEL OF PROPOSITIONS	Factual	
LEVEL OF SIGNIFIERS	He (A)	Money (O)
	Captain (A)	He (A)

Children (R)   *has stolen
Discovers
*Disappointed (att)

6

SIGNIFYING UNIT	On his return he sees a castle of gold in lovely gardens. He sees a rose arbour and remembers his promise to Beauty. He picks a rose.
LEVEL OF SEMIOSIS	The father loves his daughter very much
LEVEL OF GRAMMATICAL UNIT	Episode part (I)
LEVEL OF AFFECT SIGNIFIED	Security Selflessness
LEVEL OF RESULTS	Internal: completion External: inter-textual Internal: completion: similarity
LEVEL OF PROPOSITIONS	Action

LEVEL OF SIGNIFIERS	On his return (T)	Rose arbour (O)
	He (A)	*Promise (O)
	Castle (O)	*Beauty (R)
	Gold (att)	*Rose (O)
	Lovely (att)	sees
	Gardens (L)	remembers
	*he (A)	*picks

7

SIGNIFYING UNIT	A horrible Beast roars behind him. He has a head like a fierce animal and the body of a man. The merchant is afraid and tells his story.
LEVEL OF SEMIOSIS	2. What is going to happen next?

SIGNIFYING UNIT	1. The merchant will be punished for picking someone else's rose.
LEVEL OF GRAMMATICAL UNIT	Episode part (II)
LEVEL OF AFFECT SIGNIFIED	Insecurity
LEVEL OF RESULTS	Internal: completion External: logical
LEVEL OF PROPOSITIONS	Action Description
LEVEL OF SIGNIFIERS	Horrible (att) The body of a *Beast (A) man (att) Behind (L) +Merchant (A) Him (O) *Afraid (Att) He (A) Story (O) Like a fierce roars animal (att) tells

8

SIGNIFYING UNIT	The Beast tells the merchant he will forgive him on one condition. One daughter will come to live with him.
LEVEL OF SEMIOSIS	2. What does the Beast want with one of the merchant's daughters? 1. This is a fairy tale.
LEVEL OF GRAMMATICAL UNIT	Transition part (I)
LEVEL OF AFFECT SIGNIFIED	Selfishness v. selflessness
LEVEL OF RESULTS	External: inter-textual Internal: similarity

LEVEL OF PROPOSITIONS	Conditional Factual	
LEVEL OF SIGNIFIERS	Beast (A) Merchant (R) He (A) Him (R) *On one condition (P) *One (att)	*Daughter (O) Him (Acc) tells will forgive will come *to live with

9

SIGNIFYING UNIT	The merchant promises to tell his family. He promises to return and be the Beast's servant if they refuse.	
LEVEL OF SEMIOSIS	3. The plot is thickening 2. What will the daughters reply? 1. The father is brave, honest and protective.	
LEVEL OF GRAMMATICAL UNIT	Transition part (II)	
LEVEL OF AFFECT SIGNIFIED	Insecurity/selflessness	
LEVEL OF RESULTS	Internal: completion Internal: similarity Internal: repetition External: logical	
LEVEL OF PROPOSITIONS	Anticipatory: factual	
LEVEL OF SIGNIFIERS	*Merchant (A) To tell (O) Family (R) He (A) To return and be (O)	*The Beast's servant (O) If (conj) *promises *promises *refuse

10

SIGNIFYING UNIT	The sisters declare if Beauty had not asked for such a ridiculous present, none of these misfortunes would have happened.
LEVEL OF SEMIOSIS	Beauty is responsible for getting the father into trouble.
LEVEL OF GRAMMATICAL UNIT	Episode part (I)
LEVEL OF AFFECT SIGNIFIED	Insecurity/selfishness
LEVEL OF RESULTS	Internal: similarity External: logical
LEVEL OF PROPOSITIONS	Factual
LEVEL OF SIGNIFIERS	Sisters (A) If (conj) Beauty (A) *Such (att) *Ridiculous (att)	*Present (O) Misfortunes (O) declare None would have happened

11

SIGNIFYING UNIT	At last Beauty says she will go and live with the Beast to save her father. The father and brothers protest.
LEVEL OF SEMIOSIS	Beauty feels responsible about what she has done.
LEVEL OF GRAMMATICAL UNIT	Episode part (II)
LEVEL OF AFFECT SIGNIFIED	Insecurity Selflessness

LEVEL OF RESULTS	Internal: similarity	
LEVEL OF PROPOSITIONS	Anticipatory	
LEVEL OF SIGNIFIERS	Beauty (A) She (A) Beast (O/R) *Father (R) *To save (P)	Father (A) Brothers (A) will go and live with (at last) protest

12

SIGNIFYING UNIT	They set off and arrive at the castle which is already prepared for them. Beauty is charmed and they eat well. She almost forgets the Beast.
LEVEL OF SEMIOSIS	Things may not be so bad.
LEVEL OF GRAMMATICAL UNIT	Transition
LEVEL OF AFFECT SIGNIFIED	Hope of security
LEVEL OF RESULTS	Internal: completion External: inter-textual Internal: similarity
LEVEL OF PROPOSITIONS	Action/descriptive

LEVEL OF SIGNIFIERS	They (A) Castle (L) Which is already prepared for them (att) Beauty (A) *Charmed (att)	*They (A) well (adv) She (A) Almost (adv) Beast (R/O) set off and arrive *eat

13

| SIGNIFYING UNIT | They hear a tramp, tramp in the passage. Beauty clings to her father. The Beast growls good evening to the old man and Beauty. Beauty is frightened but replies politely. |

| LEVEL OF SEMIOSIS | But they could be. |

| LEVEL OF GRAMMATICAL UNIT | Episode part (I) |

| LEVEL OF AFFECT SIGNIFIED | Insecurity (fear) |

| LEVEL OF RESULTS | Internal: completion
Internal: similarity
External: cultural
External: logical
Internal: similarity
External: cultural |

| LEVEL OF PROPOSITIONS | Action |

| LEVEL OF SIGNIFIERS | They (A)
*Tramp, tramp (O)
Beauty (A)
Father (R)
*Beast (A)
Good evening (O)
Old man and Beauty (R) | Beauty (A)
But (conj)
Politely (adv)
Hear
*clings
*growls
replies |

14

| SIGNIFYING UNIT | The Beast asks the merchant: did Beauty come willingly? The merchant says, yes. The Beast tells him to go first thing in the morning and never |

to venture near the castle; the old man leaves, full of grief.

LEVEL OF SEMIOSIS	Why does the Beast want Beauty to be willingly there without her father?
LEVEL OF GRAMMATICAL UNIT	Episode part (II)
LEVEL OF AFFECT SIGNIFIED	Insecurity (loss)
LEVEL OF RESULTS	Internal: similarity Internal: factual Internal: similarity Internal: completion Internal: similarity
LEVEL OF PROPOSITIONS	Action
LEVEL OF SIGNIFIERS	Beast (A) Castle (L) Merchant (R) Old (att) *Beauty (A) *Man (A) *Willingly (adv) Full of grief (adv) Merchant (A) asks Yes (O) did *Beast (A) says Him (R) tells First thing in *to go the morning to venture near (T) *leaves *Never (T)

15

SIGNIFYING UNIT	One day in the garden a voice tells Beauty to be kind to the poor Beast and she will be happy.
LEVEL OF SEMIOSIS	2. Is the meaning of 'kind' in this context selflessness? 1. Fairy tales always leave a glimmer of hope.

LEVEL OF GRAMMATICAL UNIT	Event
LEVEL OF AFFECT SIGNIFIED	Hope of security
LEVEL OF RESULTS	External: inter-textual External: cultural Internal: similarity
LEVEL OF PROPOSITIONS	Factual
LEVEL OF SIGNIFIERS	One day (T) *Beast (R) In the Garden She (A) (L) *Happy (att) +Voice (A) tells *Kind (O) will be *Poor (att) to be

16

SIGNIFYING UNIT	Beauty admires the gold, dresses and jewels. The Beast seems quite gentle. He says 'good evening' and he talks nicely. She sings to him. She says she is happy at the castle but she misses her sisters, brothers, and dear father.
LEVEL OF SEMIOSIS	2. What does the Beast want with Beauty? 1. The Beast is not harmful.
LEVEL OF GRAMMATICAL UNIT	Episode part I
LEVEL OF AFFECT SIGNIFIED	Security v. insecurity (material) (separation)
LEVEL OF RESULTS	Internal: inversion Internal: similarity External: cultural; internal: sim. Internal: similarity External: cultural

LEVEL OF PROPOSITIONS	Action	
LEVEL OF SIGNIFIERS	Beauty (A) Gold (O) Dresses (O) Jewels (O) Beast (A) *quite gentle (att) He (A) *Good evening (O) He (A) Nicely (adv) She (A) Happy (A)	Castle (L) But (conj) She (A) Sisters (R) Brothers (R) *Dear (att) *Father (R) admires seems talks sings says misses

17

SIGNIFYING UNIT	The Beast asks Beauty to marry him and always live there as the mistress of the beautiful palace. Beauty says 'no', in horror. The Beast sighs and tells Beauty to have pleasant dreams.
LEVEL OF SEMIOSIS	2. But what is the meaning of marriage? 1. The meaning of being 'kind' is marrying the Beast; the meaning of kind is selfless.
LEVEL OF GRAMMATICAL UNIT	Episode part II
LEVEL OF AFFECT SIGNIFIED	Insecurity (shock/horror) Material security
LEVEL OF RESULTS	Internal: completion (S-level) External: cultural Internal: similarity; ext.: inter-textual External: cultural External: cultural

LEVEL OF PROPOSITIONS	Action	

| LEVEL OF
SIGNIFIERS | Beast (A)
Beauty (R)
*To marry (O)
Him (R)
There (L)
Beautiful (att)
Palace (O)
Beauty (A)
No (O)
Beast (A) | Beauty (R)
To have (O)
Pleasant (att)
Dreams (O)
asks
live as mistress
says in horror
sighs
tells |

18

SIGNIFYING UNIT	For some months Beauty lives in the comfort of the castle. Each evening the Beast asks Beauty to marry him. She always says 'no'. The Beast becomes sadder and sadder until Beauty feels quite sorry for him.	
LEVEL OF SEMIOSIS	2. Beauty is the cause of the Beast's distress. 1. The Beast has emotions just like a human.	
LEVEL OF AFFECT SIGNIFIED	Security v. insecurity (material) (sorrow at rejection)	
LEVEL OF RESULTS	Internal: repetition External: cultural Internal: similarity; ext.: cul.	
LEVEL OF PROPOSITIONS	Descriptive	
LEVEL OF SIGNIFIERS	For some months (T) Comfort (att) Castle (L) Beast (A) Each evening (T)	Beauty (R) To marry (O) Him (R/O) She (A) Always (adv) *No (O) *Beast (A)

*Sadder and
sadder (att)
Until (T)
*Beauty (A)
*Him (R)
lives

*says always
(adv)
becomes
*feels quite sorry
(adv)

19

SIGNIFYING UNIT	During this time Beauty often thought of her father. One day she looked into a magic mirror. She saw her father lying ill in bed. She becomes sad.
LEVEL OF SEMIOSIS	2. The father's illness brings out Beauty's kindness. 1. This is still a fairy tale.
LEVEL OF GRAMMATICAL UNIT	Transition part (I)
LEVEL OF AFFECT SIGNIFIED	Insecurity (sorrow at loss)
LEVEL OF RESULTS	Internal: similarity; ext.: cul. External: inter-textual; int.: completion Internal: factual Internal: similarity; ext.: cul.
LEVEL OF PROPOSITIONS	Factual
LEVEL OF SIGNIFIERS	During this time (T) Father (R) Beauty (A) Ill (O) Often (adv) Bed (L) Father (A) *She (A) One day (T) *Sad (att) She (A) thought †Magic (att) looked into †Mirror (O) saw She (A) lying becomes

20

SIGNIFYING UNIT	Next day Beauty asks the Beast to let her go home, for a little while, to see her father again and her brothers and sisters. The Beast is grieved as he loves Beauty so much. At last he agrees but Beauty must promise faithfully to return in two months or she may find him dead. He gives her a ring to return to the castle.
LEVEL OF SEMIOSIS	3. This is (still) a fairy tale 2. They will see each other again 1. He is really quite nice (decent)
LEVEL OF GRAMMATICAL UNIT	Transition part (II)
LEVEL OF AFFECT SIGNIFIED	Security v. insecurity (seeing the (the Beast's death) father again)
LEVEL OF RESULTS	Internal: similarity Internal: similarity Internal: similarity Internal: similarity Internal: similarity External: inter-textual Internal: completion
LEVEL OF PROPOSITIONS	Conditional
LEVEL OF SIGNIFIERS	Next day (T) Again (adv) Beauty (A) Brothers & Beast (R) Sisters (R) To let her go *Beast (A) home (P) *Grieved For a little As (Reason) while He (A) (T) Beauty (R) To see (P) *So much (adv) Her father (R) At last (adv)

He (A)	Her (R)
But (conj)	*Ring (O)
*Faithfully (adv)	To Return (P)
*To return	The Castle (L)
In two months (T)	She (A)
Or (conj)	Next morning (T)
She (S)	asks
Him (R)	loves
Dead (att)	*agrees
He (A)	*must promise
	may find
	gives
	sets out

21

SIGNIFYING UNIT	She arrives and the family is happy. Beauty runs to her father's room and, seeing her, he soon recovers. He asks if the Beast treated her kindly. After she tells her father all he wanted to know she shows Miranda and Rosina the beautiful presents she brought them and precious things for her brothers and a chest of gold for her father.
LEVEL OF SEMIOSIS	2. Everything is all right again. 1. The father was ill because he missed Beauty.
LEVEL OF GRAMMATICAL UNIT	Episode part (I)
LEVEL OF AFFECT SIGNIFIED	Security (both types) Selflessness v. selfishness
LEVEL OF RESULTS	Internal: completion Internal: similarity; ext: cul. Internal: similarity Internal: similarity; ext: cul. Internal: similarity Internal: factual

LEVEL OF PROPOSITIONS	Action	
LEVEL OF SIGNIFIERS	She (A)	*Beautiful (att)
	Family (A)	*Presents (O)
	Happy (att)	She (A)
	Beauty (A)	Them (R)
	Father's room (L)	*Precious (att)
	Her (R)	Things (O)
	Soon (adv)	Brothers (R)
	He (A)	Chest (O)
	If (prep)	*Gold (att)
	Beast (A)	Father (R)
	Her (R)	arrives
	Kindly (adv)	runs
	After (adv)	seeing
	She (A)	*recovers
	*Father (R)	asks
	All (att)	treated
	He (A)	tells
	To know (O)	wanted
	She (A)	shows
	Miranda & Rosina (R)	brought for

22

SIGNIFYING UNIT	Two happy months pass quickly. Beauty begins to think of her promise to the Beast. Her brothers beg her to stay on. She puts off going back to the castle.
LEVEL OF SEMIOSIS	Beauty is being selfish by breaking her promise to the Beast.
LEVEL OF GRAMMATICAL UNIT	Episode part (II)
LEVEL OF AFFECT SIGNIFIED	Insecurity (selfishness)
LEVEL OF RESULTS	Internal: completion Internal: similarity; ext: cul.

Internal: similarity; ext: cul.
Internal: inverse

LEVEL OF PROPOSITIONS	Factual	
LEVEL OF SIGNIFIERS	Two (att)	Her (R)
	*Happy (att)	To stay on (O)
	Months (T)	She (A)
	Quickly (adv.)	Going Back (O)
	Beauty (A)	Castle (L)
	To think (O)	pass
	*Her promise	begins
	*The Beast	beg
	†Brothers (A)	*puts off

23

SIGNIFYING UNIT	One night, Beauty has a terrible dream. The Beast is lying ill under a large tree. She hears a voice: 'You have broken your promise, Beauty, and see what has happened.' Beauty is frightened and uses the ring to go to the castle.
LEVEL OF SEMIOSIS	Beauty feels responsible for the Beast's illness.
LEVEL OF GRAMMATICAL UNIT	Transition part (I)
LEVEL OF AFFECT SIGNIFIED	Insecurity (guilt)
LEVEL OF RESULTS	Internal: inversion (the bad dream) External: cultural Internal: completion Internal: similarity; ext: cul. Internal: factual Internal: completion
LEVEL OF PROPOSITIONS	Active

| LEVEL OF SIGNIFIERS | One night (T)
Beauty (A)
Terrible (att)
Dream (O)
Beast (A)
Ill (att)
Large (att)
Tree (L)
She (A)
Voice (O)
You (A)
Your (att)
*Promise (O) | Beauty (A)
*What has
happened (O)
Beauty (A)
Frightened (att)
†Ring (I)
To go to (P)
Castle (L)
hears
*broken
*see
uses |

24

SIGNIFYING UNIT	She cannot find the Beast in the castle. At last in the evening Beauty runs into the garden weeping and calling his name. She comes to a tree, like the one in her dream. She sees the Beast lying face down, apparently dead; she is horrified. She runs for some water to revive him.
LEVEL OF SEMIOSIS	Beauty is suffering for what she has done.
LEVEL OF GRAMMATICAL UNIT	Transition part (II)
LEVEL OF AFFECT SIGNIFIED	Insecurity (anxiety)
LEVEL OF RESULTS	Internal: logical Internal: completion Internal: similarity; ext: cul. Internal: completion Internal: inversion External: logical
LEVEL OF PROPOSITIONS	Action

LEVEL OF SIGNIFIERS	She (A)	Face down (adv)
	Beast (R)	Apparently dead (att)
	Castle (L)	
	At last in the evening (T)	She (A)
		Horrified (att)
	*Beauty (A)	She (A)
	The garden (L)	For some water (O)
	*Weeping and calling (adv)	To revive him (P)
	His name (O)	cannot find
	She (A)	runs
	†Tree (L)	comes
	Like the one in her dream (comp.)	sees
		lying
	She (A)	runs
	Beast (R)	

25

SIGNIFYING UNIT	At last he opens his eyes. He is delighted to see Beauty again. He tells her he will have supper with her that night.
LEVEL OF SEMIOSIS	1. Why is he having supper with her?
	2. Beauty makes amends by saving the Beast's life!
LEVEL OF GRAMMATICAL UNIT	Episode part (I)
LEVEL OF AFFECT SIGNIFIED	Security (relief)
LEVEL OF RESULTS	Internal: completion
	Internal: similarity
	Internal: repetition
LEVEL OF PROPOSITIONS	Action
LEVEL OF SIGNIFIERS	At last (adv) Eyes (O)
	He (A) He (A)

Delighted (att)   *Supper (O)
To see (O)   Her (R)
Beauty (R)   That night (T)
Again (adv)   opens
He (A)   tells
Her (R)   *will have with
*He (A)

26

SIGNIFYING UNIT	After supper, the Beast asks Beauty to marry him. She answers 'Yes, dear Beast, I love you very much.' The Beast is surprised.
LEVEL OF SEMIOSIS	Saving his life is not enough, she also has to marry him.
LEVEL OF GRAMMATICAL UNIT	Episode part (II)
LEVEL OF AFFECT SIGNIFIED	Security (love)
LEVEL OF RESULTS	Internal: repetition Internal: similarity Internal: inversion
LEVEL OF PROPOSITIONS	Action
LEVEL OF SIGNIFIERS	After supper (T) Beast (R) Beast (A) I (A) Beauty (R) You (R) *to marry (O) asks Him (R) *answers She (A) *love very much *Yes (O) Beast (A) *Dear (O) Surprised (att)

27

SIGNIFYING UNIT	As she says this there is a tremendous flash of lightning and peal of thunder.

The ugly Beast becomes a most handsome prince standing beside Beauty. The Beast thanks Beauty for breaking a witch's spell.

LEVEL OF SEMIOSIS	2. This is Beauty's reward for making amends. 1. This is a fairy tale.
LEVEL OF GRAMMATICAL UNIT	Episode part (III)
LEVEL OF AFFECT SIGNIFIED	Security (relief)
LEVEL OF RESULTS	External: inter-textual
LEVEL OF PROPOSITIONS	Action
LEVEL OF SIGNIFIERS	As (adv) She (A) This (O) *there is a tremendous flash of lightning and peal of thunder. (Case value of scenery and special effects) Ugly (att) Beast (A) *Most handsome (att) *Prince (R) *Standing (att) *Beside (L) *Beauty (R) Beast (A) Beauty (R) Breaking a witch's spell (O) says becomes thanks

28

SIGNIFYING UNIT	Next day, the Prince sends for her father, sisters and brothers. He tells them that she promises to marry him. There is a grand wedding at the castle with many guests. They live happily ever after.
LEVEL OF SEMIOSIS	2. Everyone is happy because of Beauty's selflessness. 1. You have been reading a fairy tale.
LEVEL OF GRAMMATICAL UNIT	Ending.
LEVEL OF AFFECT SIGNIFIED	Security.
LEVEL OF RESULTS	External: cultural Internal: completion; ext: cul. External: inter-textual
LEVEL OF PROPOSITIONS	Descriptive
LEVEL OF SIGNIFIERS	Next day (T) Him (R) *Prince (A) Grand (att) Father, sisters, Castle (L) brothers (R) *with many He (A) guests (att) Them (R) They (A) She (A) *live happily ever To marry (O) after (adv.)

Appendix B
Melissa's Version of the Text

1

SIGNIFYING UNIT	The nicest daughter was Beauty and the other one, the sisters, were selfish and they always wanted to take jewels and nice dresses
LEVEL OF SEMIOSIS	2. These themes are important to me 1. This is a fairy tale
LEVEL OF GRAMMATICAL UNIT	Introduction
LEVEL OF AFFECT SIGNIFIED	Selfishness v. selflessness Material security
LEVEL OF RESULTS	External: inter-textual
LEVEL OF PROPOSITIONS	Descriptive
LEVEL OF SIGNIFIERS	*Nicest (att) Selfish (att) Daughter (A) Jewels (O) Beauty (A) Nice (att) *Other one (A) take Sisters (A) Always wanted

2

SIGNIFYING UNIT	... and but one day there was a dreadful fire.	
LEVEL OF SEMIOSIS	Sometimes in fairy tales terrible things happen.	
LEVEL OF GRAMMATICAL UNIT	Event	
LEVEL OF AFFECT SIGNIFIED	Insecurity	
LEVEL OF RESULTS	External: inter-textual	
LEVEL OF PROPOSITIONS	Factual	
LEVEL OF SIGNIFIERS	†And (conj) †But (conj) One day (T)	*Dreadful (att) Fire (O)

3

SIGNIFYING UNIT	and so somebody called to the man ... the ... um ... father; to go on, um, a ship with cargoes.
LEVEL OF SEMIOSIS	2. The man is also a father 1. Fairy tales offer a glimmer of hope
LEVEL OF GRAMMATICAL UNIT	Transition
LEVEL OF AFFECT SIGNIFIED	Hope of security
LEVEL OF RESULTS	External: inter-texual

LEVEL OF PROPOSITIONS	Anticipatory	
LEVEL OF SIGNIFIERS	†And (conj) †So (conj) †Somebody (A) *Man ... the ... um ... father (R)	Um ship (O) With cargoes (att) called to go on

4

SIGNIFYING UNIT	... and the daughters ... when he ... the daughters had to do all the cleaning and the washing up because they had to move in a small, little cottage.	
LEVEL OF SEMIOSIS	1. Washing up without protest is being a nice girl.	
LEVEL OF GRAMMATICAL UNIT	Event	
LEVEL OF AFFECT SIGNIFIED	Insecurity	
LEVEL OF RESULTS	Internal: completion Internal: completion	
LEVEL OF PROPOSITIONS	Factual	
LEVEL OF SIGNIFIERS	And (conj) The daughters (A) †When (R) He (A) The daughters (A) *All the cleaning	And the washing (O) Because (conj) They (A) In a small, little (att) Cottage (O) had to do had to move in

5

SIGNIFYING UNIT	I think he got a rose
LEVEL OF SEMIOSIS	1. The father loves his daughter very much
LEVEL OF GRAMMATICAL UNIT	Episode part I
LEVEL OF AFFECT SIGNIFIED	Security
LEVEL OF RESULTS	External: cultural Internal: completion
LEVEL OF PROPOSITIONS	Action
LEVEL OF SIGNIFIERS	I (A) think *He (A) got *Rose (O)

6

SIGNIFYING UNIT	and he got into trouble with the Beast.
LEVEL OF SEMIOSIS	1. He stole the rose from the Beast
LEVEL OF GRAMMATICAL UNIT	Episode part II
LEVEL OF AFFECT SIGNIFIED	Insecurity
LEVEL OF RESULTS	External: cultural

LEVEL OF PROPOSITIONS	Action

LEVEL OF SIGNIFIERS	†And (conj) *He got into trouble with (idiomatic) the Beast (A)

7

SIGNIFYING UNIT	and he asked her ... um ... him to let Beauty ... um come to him ... and so she ... um ... came

LEVEL OF SEMIOSIS	2. The father and daughter are separated by the sister 1. The father and daughter are inseparable

LEVEL OF GRAMMATICAL UNIT	Transition

LEVEL OF AFFECT SIGNIFIED	Insecurity

LEVEL OF RESULTS	Internal: future External: inter-textual

LEVEL OF PROPOSITIONS	Action

LEVEL OF SIGNIFIERS	And (conj) She (A) He (A) asked *Her (R) to let Him (R) um come to Beauty (R) um came And so (conj)

8

SIGNIFYING UNIT	But she broke a promise when she saw her father ill and she said she'd come back after two months but she didn't

LEVEL OF SEMIOSIS	1. Beauty breaks the promise because of father's illness
LEVEL OF GRAMMATICAL UNIT	Event
LEVEL OF AFFECT SIGNIFIED	Selfish
LEVEL OF RESULTS	External : cultural
LEVEL OF PROPOSITIONS	Factual
LEVEL OF SIGNIFIERS	†But (conj) After 2 months She (A) (T) A promise (O) But (conj) When (T) She (A) She (A) broke Her (att) saw †Father (att) said *Ill (att) would come back She (A) didn't

9

SIGNIFYING UNIT	... and so um she dreamed that she saw um Beast um dead under a large tree and when she went there she did and then there was thunder and he woke up.
LEVEL OF SEMIOSIS	2. I love my father but mother is a problem 1. This is a fairy tale
LEVEL OF GRAMMATICAL UNIT	Event
LEVEL OF AFFECT SIGNIFIED	Excitement Insecurity

LEVEL OF RESULTS	External: inter-textual Internal: completion	

LEVEL OF PROPOSITIONS	Factual	

LEVEL OF SIGNIFIERS	And so (conj) †Um she (A) Um Beast (O/R) Um dead (Att) Under a large Tree (L) And when (T) She (A) There (L) She (A)	And then (conj) Thunder (O) And (conj) He (A) dreamed saw went *did woke up

10

SIGNIFYING UNIT	... and they had a wedding	

LEVEL OF SEMIOSIS	2. The situation is not entirely happy 1. This is a fairy tale	

LEVEL OF GRAMMATICAL UNIT	Ending	

LEVEL OF AFFECT SIGNIFIED	Happiness	

LEVEL OF RESULTS	External: inter-textual Internal: completion	

LEVEL OF PROPOSITIONS	Factual	

LEVEL OF SIGNIFIERS	And (conj) They (A)	A wedding (O)

Appendix C
Interview with Melissa

Melissa's text

The nicest daughter was Beauty and the other *one*, the sisters were selfish and they always wanted to take jewels; and nice dresses. And but one day ... there was a dreadful fire and so somebody called to the man ... the um father to go on um a ship with cargoes. And the daughters ... when he ... the daughters had to do all the cleaning and the washing up because they had to move in a small, little cottage.

(She has a pause here; I encourage her to try and remember what happens after that.)

I think he got a rose and he got into trouble with the Beast and he asked her um him to let Beauty um come to him and so she um came. But she broke a promise when she saw her father ill and she said she'd come back after two months but she didn't and so um she dreamed that she saw um beast um dead under a large tree and when she went there she did and then there was thunder and he woke up and they had a wedding.

Interview

1. Who is your favourite character in the story/favourite person?
'I like the father best.'
2. Why?
'Well, he was kind and he got what they wanted.'
3. He got?
'What Beauty wanted, and he wasn't cruel.'
4. And who do you like least in that story?
'Alioese' (not comprehensible), I didn't like the sisters.'

5. Why weren't they very nice?
'Well, when they did the washing up they grumbled; and Beauty didn't, she just did it.'
6. Do you do the washing up here?
'Sometimes.'
7. Do you grumble when you do it?
'I ask Mummy if I can do it.'
8. And do you think that Beauty did the washing up?
'Yes.'
9. What does Beauty look like?
'Um, she's got fair hair and she's got blue eyes, and she has a sort of um necklace round there and she has um blue eyes and ...'
10. What kind of clothes does she wear?
'She wears a silver sort of dress and um black.'
11. Does the sister remind you of anyone?
'... One of Cinderella's sisters.'
12. Does this story remind you of Cinderella and in what way?
'They wanted lots of clothes and they grumbled and they did the washing up but they didn't do it. Cinderella had a kind father as well ... and like she just had a wicked sort of mother, but she hasn't got one, you see.'
13. Does it remind you of any other fairy tales you have read?
'Snow White maybe but I'm not sure about that because she hasn't got two sisters.'
14. But why Snow White?
'Well, because she was like Cinderella and um (correcting herself) Beauty because she was kind to the animals and she did the washing up in the dwarves' house.'
15. Does your brother do the washing up or is he too small?
'Too small.'
16. Who is your second favourite character in this story?
'Beauty.'
17. And who is the third most?
'I don't know.'
18. Do you like the Beast?
'Yes.'
19. Why do you like him?
'Well, he wasn't sort of powerful, he was nice, he didn't ... he wasn't horrible to Beauty.'
20. What do you think is the most exciting event in this story?
'When she had to go to the Beast and when she dreamt that he was dead.'
21. Why do you think the witch put a wicked spell on the Beast?
'... (long pause) cause I think that it was like Rapunzel: when he, she had maybe the witch had a daughter and he was trying to

get her but she found out and so she, the witch, put a spell on him.'

22. Do you think that Beauty has ever been naughty in her life?
'Naughty? ... (long pause) ... No.'
23. If this story were written without the father would you still want to read it?
'Well, not really.'
24. Do you think the father was good?
'Yes.'
25. Is that why you like him best?
'Yes.'
26. How did you feel when he had to send his daughter to the Beast?
'I felt sorry for him.'
27. Him?
'And Beauty, maybe she didn't want to go and I don't think he wanted her to go. But I think that the sisters wanted her to go because they didn't like her.'
28. Why were they against Beauty?
'Because they said, when she wanted a rose, she said it was ridiculous, to have a rose, but I thought it was all right; I'd like a rose.'
29. Is a rose your favourite flower?
'Yes.'
30. Do you have roses in the garden?
'Yes.'
31. Do you get roses from your garden?
'No.'
32. Aren't you allowed to have them?
'No, I do have some plants; I give the roses to my teacher at school.'
33. How do you think the brothers felt, when Beauty had to leave?
'I think they felt sad, they were nice like Beauty and they weren't selfish.'
34. When she came back they didn't want her to go did they? Why?
'I think they'd been sad because she went and they just liked her and missed her so they wanted her to stay a little bit longer.'
35. Who was doing the washing up when Beauty left?
'Um ... I think the sisters ... had to.'
36. Would the brothers?
'I don't think so.'
37. How did you feel at the end of the story?
'Uh ... I felt happy ... (Laugh) ...'
38. For whom?
'For Beauty and the Prince.'

39. And anybody else?
'Yes, for the father . . . because I think he wanted her to marry.'
40. Who would you leave out if you could leave someone out?
'I'd leave out one of the sisters.'
41. Which one?
'Um . . . the one who wanted the ruby necklace.'
42. Why?
'Well, because it's expensive.'
43. And you think she's greedy do you?
'Yes.'
44. And who else would you leave out and still like the story?
'Um . . . the other sister.'
45. No one else?
'No.'
46. (Drawing commenced for about ten minutes. The first drawing was of the sister who wanted the necklace)
Why are you drawing the sister first?
'I think she's the easiest one.'
47. She's not the prettiest, is she?
'No.'
48. What part of that story would you now like to put into pictures?
(She now draws the scene of the dead Beast with lightning in the sky, i.e. the Beast is both dead and being reborn.)
49. What scene is this you are drawing now?
'When he's dead under the large tree, with lightning.'
50. When does that lightning happen in the story?
'I think when he's dead.'
51. If you read this story again what would you add? To make it more enjoyable?
'I'd say that they lived in the castle and that . . . um . . . the sisters made friends with Beauty.'
52. What do you think his name is, besides Prince?
'Prince Andrew.'
53. Where do you think his parents are?
'In a palace.'
54. Not in his palace?
'No.'
55. How do you think he can change into a handsome man?
'I think she just . . . um . . . I don't know . . . (laugh).'
56. Why did you stop reading fairy tales?
'Well, I thought they were a bit young for me so I felt I was going to read older books.'
57. What is your second most favourite fairy tale?
'*The Miller's Daughter*. And she had to spin the thread into gold.'

58. Why is it your favourite?

'Because it's sort of exciting ... when she, you think she can't do it all in one night, but it's exciting when that little man comes in and helps her, and in the end he says what will you give and *I* haven't ... and she says I've got nothing to give you and so he says when you grow will you give me your young, but she didn't want to give her young.'

I also got her description of the important event of the Beast under the tree, dead. Her favourite scene remains the Beast lying under the tree even though she seems aware of the fact that Beauty broke the spell. Asked why, she said that 'it's just a good scene.'

59. Description of the father in the story.

'He has grey hair, kind face, brown boots, green suit.'

60. Description of mother:

'She's dead, had a kind face, a red dress, yellow hair, red shoes and a rose was her favourite flower.' (Her mother's favourite flower is a lily.)

61. Description of your father.

'Kind, strong and generous.'

62. Which one of Cinderella's sisters did you dislike?

'The one who has a black dress, lots of clothes, is nasty, small nose (the nose is in fact very big), black hair and shoes.'

63. What is your teacher like?

'She has grey curly hair, wears a patterned dress – kind – kind face, pretty, old, like gramma.'

64. Why is this sister in the story easy to draw?

'The other is too complicated.'

65. Who has the most clothes in the family?

'I do.'

Bibliography

Anderson, J. R. (1976), *Language, Memory and Thought*, New York, Halsted.

Anderson, J. R. and Bower, G. H. (1973), *Human Associative Memory*, New York, Halsted.

Barthes, R. (1970), *S/Z*, Paris, Senil.

Barthes, R. (1972), 'The Structuralist Activity', in the *Structuralists from Marx to Lévi-Strauss*, Richard and Fernande De George (eds), New York, Doubleday.

Barthes, R. (1973), *Mythologies*, trans. Annette Lavers, London, Paladin.

Barthes, R. (1977), *Elements of Semiology*, trans. Annette Lavers and Colin Smith, New York, Hall & Wang.

Bartlett, F. C. (1932), *Remembering*, Cambridge U.P.

Benveniste, E. (1971), *Problems in General Linguistics*, trans. Mary Elizabeth Meek, University of Miami Press.

Bettelheim, B. (1978), *The Uses of Enchantment, The Meaning of Fairy Tales*, Harmondsworth, Penguin.

Bloomfield, L. (1933), *Language*, New York, Holt, Rhinehart & Winston.

Bowlby, J. (1969), *Attachment and Loss I: Attachment*, London, Hogarth.

Bransford, J. D. and Franks, J. J. (1972), 'The Abstraction of Linguistic Ideas: A Review', *Cognition: An International Journal of Psychology*. **2**, 24–249.

Chandler, R. (1958), *Playback*, Harmondsworth, Penguin.

Culler, J. (1976), *Saussure*, Glasgow, Fontana/Collins.

Culler, J. (1975), *Structuralist Poetics; Structuralism, Linguistics and the Study of Literature*, London, Routledge & Kegan Paul.

Dunker, (1972), *On Problem Solving*, trans. L. S. Kes, Westpoint, Conn., Greenwood Press.

Eco, Umberto. (1977), *A Theory of Semiotics*, London, Macmillan.
Empson, W. (1965), *Seven Types of Ambiguity*, London, Penguin Books.
Evans-Pritchard, E. E. (1951), *Social Anthropology*, London, Calper West.
Fillmore, C. J. (1968). *The Case for Case*, in E. Bach and R. T. Harms (eds), *Universals in Linguistic Theory*, New York, Holt, Rhinehart & Winston.
Flaubert, G. (1970), *Madame Bovary*, trans. Alan Russell, London, Penguin.
Freud, S. (1900), *The Interpretation of Dreams*, S. E., vol. V.
Freud, S. (1905), *Three Essays on the Theory of Sexuality*, S.E. vol. VII.
Freud, S. (1974), *Introductory Lectures*, Harmondsworth, Penguin.
Gibson, J. J. (1966), *The Senses Considered as Perceptual Systems*, Boston, Houghton Mifflin Co.
Goertz, C. (1979), *An Ethnography of the Disciplines*, Eminent Lectures Series, BIOSS, Brunel University.
Harre, R. (1974), 'The Conditions for a Social Psychology of Childhood', in *The Integration of a Child into the Social World*, Martin P. M. and Richards (ed.) Cambridge University Press.
Hjelmslev, L. (1961), *Prolegomena to a Theory of Language*, trans. Whitfield, F. J., Madison, University of Wisconsin Press.
Jakobson, R. (1978), *Six Lectures on Sound and Meaning*, trans. John Mepham, Hassocks, Harvester Press.
Jakobson, R. and Halle, M. (1971), *Fundamentals of Language*, The Hague, Mouton.
Jameson, F. (1972), *The Prison House of Language*, Princeton, N.J., Princeton University Press.
Kintsch, W. (1974), *The Representation of Meaning in Memory*, Hillsdale, N.J., Lawrence Erlbaum Associates.
Klein, G. S. (1972), *Freud's Two Theories of Sexuality* in Berger, L. (ed.) *Clinical and Cognitive Psychology*, Englewood Cliffs, N.J. Prentice-Hall.
Kuhn, T. S. (1970), *The Structure of Scientific Revolutions: International Encyclopaedia of Unified Science*, London, University of Chicago Press.
Lacan, J. (1966), *Ecrits*, Paris, Senil.
Lacan, J. (1972), *The Insistence of the Letter in the Unconscious or Reason since Freud*, in De George, R. and De George F. (eds), *The Structuralists from Marx to Lévi-Strauss*, New York, Doubleday.
Laplanche, J. and Pontalis, J. B. (1973), *The Language of Psycho-analysis*, London: Hogarth Press and the Institute of Psycho-Analysis.

Leach, E. (1964), '*Anthropological Aspects of Language:* Animal Categories and Verbal Abuse', in *New Directions in the Study of Language* (ed.) Lenneberg, E. A., MIT Press, pp. 23–63.

Leach, E. (1970), *Lévi Strauss*, London, Fontana/Collins.

Lévi-Strauss, C. (1970), *The Raw and the Cooked*, trans. John & Doreen Weightman, London, Jonathan Cape.

Lévi-Strauss, C. (1972), 'The Structural Study of Myth and Four Winnebago Myths', in Richard and Fernande De George (eds), *The Structuralist from Marx to Lévi-Strauss*, New York, Doubleday.

Lindsay, P. H. and Norman, D. H. (1972), *Human Information Processing: Introduction to Psychology*, London, Academic Press.

Lyons, J. (1970), *Chomsky*, London, Fontana/Collins.

Mandle, G. (1975), *Mind and Emotion*, London, Wiley.

Minnis, N. (ed.) (1973), *Linguistics at Large*, London, Paladin.

Miranda, P. (ed.) (1972), *Mythology*, London, Penguin.

Newell, A., & Simon, H. A. (1972), *Human Problem Solving*, Englewood Cliffs, N.J., Prentice-Hall.

Pettit, P. (1975), *The Concept of Structuralism: A Critical Analysis*, Dublin, Gill & Macmillan.

Piaget, J. (1971), *Structuralism*, trans. Chaninah Maschlek, London: Routledge & Kegan Paul.

Propp, V. (1968), *Morphology of the Folktale*, trans. Laurence Scott, London, University of Texas Press.

Putnam, H. (1971), 'On Reductionism', *Cognition*.

Richards, M. P. M. (ed.) (1974), *The Integration of a Child into a Social World*, Cambridge University Press.

Sandler, J. and Sandler, A.-M. (1978), 'On the Development of Object Relationships and Affects', *International Journal of Psycho-Analysis*, 59, 205.

Saussure, F. De. (1974), *Course in General Linguistics*, trans. Wade Baskin, Glasgow, Fontana/Collins.

Schachter, S. (1971), *Emotion, Obesity and Crime*, New York, Academic Press.

Trilling, D. (1978), 'The Liberated Heroine', *Times Literary Supplement*, London, October.

Ullmann, S. (1973), *Meaning and Style*, Oxford, Blackwell.

Index